Becoming Fluent in the
LANGUAGE
of Content

Developing Strategic Readers As Critical Consumers of Information

2, 3, 5, 7, 11, 13, 17, 19, 23, 29, 31, 37, 41, 43, 47, 53, 59, 61, 67, 71, 73, 79, 83, 89, 97

LORY HAAS | PATRICIA DURHAM | JOAN WILLIAMS

Kendall Hunt
publishing company

Cover image © Shutterstock, Inc.

Kendall Hunt
publishing company

www.kendallhunt.com
Send all inquiries to:
4050 Westmark Drive
Dubuque, IA 52004-1840

Contents

Introduction

> *Education is not the filling of a pail, but the lighting of a fire.*
> *—William Butler Yeats*

Such few words, yet such profound meaning. Isn't that what we as educators really want to do—light a fire in our students and develop their passion for learning? Have you ever watched children playing outside and noted their observations and interactions with their environment? What about the endless questions they have when riding in a car, going to the grocery store, the park, or any other outing? Then, there is that infamous one-word question, "*Why*?" that children love to ask repeatedly. Children are very inquisitive and want to experience and learn about the world around them and in today's world vast amounts of information can be readily accessed with the touch of a finger. Answers to questions can be found quickly, but of course not everything can be answered; some questions can lead to more inquiry and critical thinking.

Information and nonfiction **is** the world we live in; however, the genre of choice for most primary classrooms is fiction. So where does this leave the "info kids," children who are not interested in stories that begin with, *Once upon a time...* or flat, one-dimensional characters with little to no depth in personality? Some children thirst for information and want to read, hear, and experience nonfiction. Furthermore, all children need adequate access and exposure to a variety of informational texts. They need to develop fluency in new media literacies where they learn to read critically, explore, analyze, and synthesize information. This requires students to become critical consumers of information, looking through a critical lens and making informed decisions about text.

Information in today's world is more readily available than ever before and information on virtually any topic can be accessed with the touch of a finger. However, not all information that is accessible is credible or at times even true. With the vast amount of information available and new forms of media as an everyday part of our lives, we must evaluate what skills and strategies students need to become fluent readers of information. Teachers must plan and implement authentic opportunities to help students become critical thinkers, which will better equip them for lifelong success. To do so, effective teachers must have knowledge, specifically:

KNOWLEDGE OF CLASSROOM ENVIRONMENTS THAT SUPPORT CONTENT AREA LEARNING

- Setting purposes for content area learning.
- Organizing instructional environment for specific instructional objectives and optimal learning opportunities.
- Instructional methods and strategies to integrate the five literacies across the curriculum and content subject areas (e.g., modeling, scaffolding, exploration and discovery, explicit, and systematic instruction).
- Implement effective techniques to support students' interests, abilities, increase engagement, and improve attitudes toward content area reading.

KNOWLEDGE OF ASSESSING STUDENT INTERESTS, ABILITIES, AND INSTRUCTIONAL MATERIALS

- Appropriately assessing individual student reading levels and literacy development.
- Evaluating readers and matching instructional materials to students' interests of topics and genres at their reading level.
- Implementing appropriate methods for meeting reading and learning needs of diverse learners.

KNOWLEDGE OF COMPONENTS OF READING COMPREHENSION

- Elements of reading comprehension (e.g., author's purpose and background/prior knowledge).
- Strategies to facilitate students' reading comprehension (e.g., inferring, predicting, summarizing, monitoring, generating questions, semantic and graphic organizers)
- Strategies for reading comprehension and content learning through digital literacies.

- Instructional strategies to increase vocabulary acquisition (e.g., context clues, use of text features, and word analysis).
- Strategies for developing critical thinking (e.g., metacognition, analysis, synthesis, evaluation).
- Connections between text and self, text to text, and text to world.

KNOWLEDGE OF CONTENT SPECIFIC LEARNING THROUGH THE FIVE LITERACIES

- Author's use of text structures (e.g., descriptive, cause and effect, problem/solution, sequential order, compare and contrast)
- Features of non-fiction texts (e.g., side bars, index, bolded words, headings/subheadings, glossary,) to support learning of content.
- Instructional approaches and strategies for learning through digital literacies using the TPACK model.
- Instructional approaches and strategies for acquiring content area vocabulary (e.g., word walls, graphic organizers, categorizing, semantic mapping, and semantic feature analysis).
- Purposeful selection and evaluation of print and non-print media and materials for instructional purposes.
- Instructional strategies and approaches for discovery learning circles and inquiry for both traditional and digital texts (e.g., note taking skills; summarizing; discussion; using text features, such as illustrations, maps, and graphics).
- Instructional approaches and strategies to assist students in developing fluency in the language of content.
- Instructional approaches and strategies for helping students with inquiry, research, gathering, evaluating, analyzing, synthesizing, and sharing information.

As you can see teachers need much knowledge in providing effective instructional opportunities to all students. Informational texts and new media literacies open new doors for our students and for us as teachers. We must enter those doors with a willingness to explore new texts, think more critically, question, and travel the journey of learning with our students in new and different ways. We need to foster an environment of inquiry for students and ourselves as educators. The goal of our text is to provide information to guide you in creating authentic learning experiences that help students become fluent in the language of content and critical consumers of information.

Keep these few but powerful words in mind as you embark on this journey.

"Children must be taught how to think, not what to think."
— Margaret Mead

SECTION I
Acquiring the Language of Content

$E = MC^2$

$\pi = 3.14159265$

$v_f = v_i + at$

$a^2 + b^2 = c^2$

H_2O

?

x

5 cm

90

$M = 5.9736 \times 10^{24}$ kg

2, 3, 5, 7, 11, 13, 17, 19, 23, 29, 31, 37, 41, 43, 47, 53, 59, 61, 67, 71, 73, 79, 83, 89, 97

Chapter One

Developing a Framework for Thinking about Content as Language

Teaching...can be likened to a conversation in which you listen to the speaker carefully before you reply. --Marie Clay

As humans, we are very social creatures, and at the center of this society is our language. To be interactive with society we naturally embrace a journey to acquiring language—we want to communicate about the wonders and sights around us! From birth we babble, mimic, and listen to those who are experts with language. Then we experiment with what we hear realizing there are patterns to language and begin to string along ideas until we eventually master the cognitive, oral, and written aspect of our language, using it to grow in our understanding of society.

Although language may take on multiple identities, for our purposes, the process of becoming fluent in the language of **content** involves acquiring the **five literacies** of language. When we can read, write, speak, think, and listen in a language, we can truly use that language to interact with others in our society. In the society of a classroom, content is simply another language, the student is a "second language content learner," and the teacher a "content language teacher." Yet many approaches to teaching content overlook highlighting the importance of truly becoming fluent in the language of content. Developing a **metacognitive** awareness by both teachers and students for all five literacies sets a new lens for looking at how we teach our students about the acquisition for the *language* of science, social studies, mathematics, and other content-related fields. By not addressing content as a language we risk portraying that the learning of content is merely the acquisition of facts, rather than an acquired language that students can use to learn and grow in their understanding of the society that uses that language—even if that society is in their very own classrooms. With the amount of information available at our fingertips, we must implement 21st-century skills for students to become critical consumers of information and analytical thinkers.

The Five Literacies of the 21st Century

Around the turn of the 21st century, a new term began showing up in conversations about children. The so-called Net-gen or Net-generation was being used to explain that "modern 'kids' are spending their early years in an environment that differs fundamentally from that of their parents" as they are connected and have access to an array of information found on the internet (Millard, 2003, p. 5). These children experience literacy in ways that were not accessible in previous generations. From visual to interactive, literacy is no longer just about reading and writing. This new generation of learners requires a new generation of teachers who understand that learners function on a multidimensional stage. Literacy is the social interaction between reading, writing, speaking, and listening to create understanding. In addition, this meaning of literacy also includes the *ways* of "thinking, believing, feeling, valuing, acting/doing and interacting in relation" to the context AND content around them. Children in the Net-generation use literacy to form communities of learners outside the classroom (e.g., social media, video gaming, ebooks, internet exploring, interactive television) (Gee, 1989; Knobel & Lankshear, 2007, p. 3). Now, imagine what that looks like inside the classroom! It is most likely a very different image of the classroom you were in! As teachers, we want learners to constantly use these literacies to be reflective about their context and content. We want them to respond to literature and learning, and to realize and vocalize when learning amazes them (WOW), when they "get it" (Ah-ha), and when they want to know more (Wonder). While those may seem to be common responses to literature or fiction, it is important to realize that **informational text** or **nonfiction** *is* the literature of fact.

Becoming a "content language" teacher focuses on helping students become fluent speakers, readers, writers, thinkers, and listeners of this new "language called content." Such a teacher first creates a classroom society where students are curious about knowledge and where they become aware of the benefits the five literacies have for owning this knowledge. This teacher then helps students fill that metaphorical "content language toolbox" full of strategies that develop each of the literacies to aid in both current and future learning of content language.

Acquisition of Content Language through the Five Literacies

Reading. It is a common misconception that if one knows how to read, then one can read any genre. It is a greater misconception to think that teaching how to read ends in the lower elementary grades. In an era where **text complexity** has become the buzz word for the field of reading, teaching "how to read" becomes never-ending as text complexity is unique to each reader and each text. What may be a fluent read for one student may be complex for other readers based on their interests, level, background, and exposure to multiple genres. Think about taking a biology course—possibly the one you took during your first few years of college. For you, as an education major, that was not quite everyday language. To become fluent in the content language of biology, you would need to reassess how you navigate the content. The reading of that text will require you to read slower due to vocabulary that is not yet a "language" for you. It will require you to reread to build connection to the text. It will involve you to possibly "zig-zag" through the text to cross-reference knowledge from other sections of the text. For you, the text complexity is high as it is a foreign language to you. Now, think about pre-med majors who are submerged in the language of biology. The text complexity is more easily negotiable. The "language of the content" has become more fluent for them as they have had more access to the primer for that language based on background. They will not need to cross-reference as much, reread sections as often, or refer to other reference sources to navigate the text. For them, the text complexity is low as the text connects to a familiar language system.

The complexity of a text requires readers to adjust and readjust how they navigate through the text. It requires them to assess how much support they are going to need to build their understanding for the text. Without this knowledge, a reader of **content text** or **nonfiction** may become frustrated and discouraged resulting in withdrawal of an authentic content language acquisition process. Text complexity too often gets confused with proficient readers. Proficient readers of fiction often assume they can read anything, and teachers sometimes assume that proficient readers can handle all text levels. It is important to keep in mind that reading strategies students have developed and used to comprehend fiction do not necessarily help them understand content text. When they encounter difficulty reading content/informational text as a result of using fiction strategies rather than content text strategies, they may question their ability and give up trying to read the text. Think about an experience reading content or informational text at a high text complexity level. How did it make you feel? How did you react to it? Part of unlocking informational text is for content language learners to develop expectations for the differences between genres. It is important for readers to know that when one reads fiction, it is expected for the work to be untrue, have the specific elements of a story, read from front to back, begin at the top of a page, and be guided by the plot of the structure. For nonfiction or informational text the expectations are quite different. Readers expect what is read to be true and accurate. It may be read as a whole or in parts based on the needs of the reader. Readers of informational text will utilize the **navigational tools** developed by the author by accessing the visual elements such as graphics or other features of content-based text.

While the foundation of *how* to read may have been established in the early elementary years, content language teachers must be equipped to teach students how to use those skills to navigate a diverse array of content text. In the 21st century, content text or **informational text** can be traditional hard-copy text, digital text, visual text, and multimedia-based text. If students are to be prepared to become fluent in the content they are learning, teachers of that content language will need to establish the "Rosetta stone" for acquiring that language. What is the structure of the content text? How will they unlock that structure to access the text? How has the author assisted the reader to unlock the text? How do we navigate as a reader of content text? These are questions readers will need to ask to support themselves to acquire content knowledge through reading.

No, teaching *how* to read does not end in the early elementary grades, it just becomes more focused on the language of the content, the structure of the text, and the ability to bridge that to the other five literacies of becoming fluent in the language of content. What is absolutely certain is that without reading *about* content, students can struggle to become fluent in the content they are learning. It must be part of the learning process rather than assigned in the background. A common reason why "reading" is not included in the acquisition of content on a regular basis is because "the text is too difficult to read." Our 21st-century students just cannot afford for us to treat content reading that way. As a content language teacher, you will need to embed your lessons with strategies that will teach students how to access the text so they can navigate the complexity of the text independently. For if we do not provide experiences with content texts at all levels we do them a disservice, as students will not learn how to navigate them for later years in the middle and high school grades when the amount of content text increases.

Writing. Take a moment and think about your earliest writing experiences with content text. Wait, let me guess! It was the research report that ended up glued to a poster board and presented at the front of the class. Now, think about writing in the 21st century! What does it look like? How do we use it? When you read something off the internet, does it look like a five-paragraph essay? When you look in a DK book such as *Volcanoes,* what are you drawn to? If we want students to become fluent in the language of their content, we need them to write authentically and for a purpose. Why and how do informational text authors write? What are the modes that they write in?

A common misconception about writing content text is that if a student knows how to write, then the student can write in any genre. It probably doesn't need to be said, but that is just not the case. So far, we have discussed that to become fluent in the language of content, students must be engaged readers of that content. If as readers we "read to listen" to an author, then we need students to understand that authors "write to be heard" and the relationship between these two literacies supports the acquisition of the content language being learned. As a content literacy teacher, you will need to study the **genres of informational text** and their structures. If we want students to be writers of the 21st century, we are going to need to provide them with authentic text as models. Using **mentor text**, teachers can bridge *how* to write with *why* authors write, to help establish a purpose for writing. It is not enough for students to read about a content subject, but to really become fluent in that content the acquisition process must extend to sharing this knowledge with an audience. They need to be able to use the language of the content to communicate this understanding in text form. And with that said, the more students read informational text, the more they become accustomed to the structure and purpose for it. There is a significant gain in acquisition of the content language and of understanding by connecting these two literacies. It is known that when second language learners have multiple exposures to text this develops a familiarity of the structure and of the use of the written language which can prepare them for their own writing (Farnan, Flood, & Lapp, 1994). By studying the relationship between the text which is written and the text that *will* be written, students build a personal investment in the learning of the content while constructing understanding of how the knowledge of that content is used as a language both written and read.

It is important to point out that just like reading in the 21st century extends past the hard-copy text form, so too should the platforms for student writ-

AUTHENTIC WRITING MENTOR TEXT/MULTIGENRE MODES

- Advertisement
- eNewspaper/eArticle
- Magazine
- Website
- Blog
- Email notice
- Diary perspective
- Script writing/ reenactment
- Mock award nomination
- School/classroom newsletter
- School/classroom/library Indi-book publishing
- "Weekly-Reader/Time for Kids-like" publication
- Interview summary
- Game rule
- Wanted posters
- Diaries

ing. Students encounter informational text on a daily basis outside of the classroom but when we ask them to write in that traditional five-paragraph essay format, a disconnect develops. It is stale to them and unauthentic as it lacks the qualities of the informational text of their time. Students come to expect outside-of-classroom content knowledge to be presented in a certain way. The *Gamer* or *American Girl* magazine that students might read today presents content knowledge with numerous navigational tools or **access features** to help the reader navigate through the text. The look and feel of the content allows them to travel through the knowledge, building a connection with the text. For students to become fluent in the language of content, they will need to deconstruct and construct their written knowledge in a fashion that connects with the 21st century. As a content language teacher, you will need to embed your lessons with models, demonstrations, and opportunities that will teach students how to transfer content learned into knowledge communicated in written form. Real-world informational text writing may look very different from your "research paper or presentation" of the past but it becomes vital for 21st-century teachers to offer a variety of authentic writing platforms in **multigenre modes** in which students can bridge out-of-classroom informational text with in-classroom learning (see Appendix for an extended list).

Speaking. Ask teachers about students' abilities to speak, and they will hands down say students have definitely mastered that task... just not in the academic setting! There lies the problem! Students' speaking skills are vital for 21st-century teachers to capitalize on! Children are natural conversationalists, and if we give appropriate structure to communicate and use content language to extend learning we help them satisfy that natural trait. The more we can allow students to "talk" or discuss about what they *think* they know related to a content, the more they will confirm or extend that knowledge as their learning continues. Becoming fluent in the language of content means as teachers we need students not just to read and write, but to *use* that language in appropriate conversation contexts.

Let's step back and think about how we acquired our first language of communication. As babies, we babbled and mimicked language parts to communicate and have needs met. We received praise with claps and smiles for our efforts even if we missed the mark on the attempt. Some oral language development theories describe young children in the early school years as in a stage of experimentation with language. Parts of speech may be used correctly or incorrectly, but during this time language learners try out ways of using language to learn about the world around them and for interacting with society in acceptable ways (Tompkins, 2005). Now, let's take that thinking into the content classroom society. If we continue to think of our students as acquiring a second language of content, we need to make connections to how the first language was acquired. Similar opportunities should

BECOMING FLUENT IN THE LANGUAGE OF CONTENT

be provided to explore the ways one can use the various terms and expressions of the content language to experiment and use content language to interact with society (the classroom) in acceptable academic ways. It is very important for us to provide a **communicative purpose** for learning content so that learners can negotiate understanding with others who use the same language based on something they heard, read, or wrote. The old saying, "If you don't use it, you will lose it!" applies quite nicely to content language acquisition. If we do not have students interact with the spoken language of content, we risk the chance that the content knowledge becomes short- lived and possibly never becomes part of their working vocabulary.

Alright, so we want students to talk about what they are learning. Be very cautious of taking a stance that just because they can communicate to you using "*a*" language, students will then be able to use that language to communicate content. Planned opportunities to discuss content in both formal and informal context settings will allow students to build their **content fluency** but they need to know what that looks and sounds like first. What is the authentic purpose for speaking in that content language? What does it sound like to be a scientist, a mathematician, a musician, an artist, a historian, or any other content field students may encounter during their school years? How are the terms and concepts of that content used in the society of that **lexicon**? How do we casually talk about something we have learned? How do we defend our understanding in more formal debate scenarios? …Do you get the idea? **Mentor speech** is just as vital for learning how to use the content language as mentor text is to learning how to write. As teachers, we have access to recorded video or audio of authentic speakers to use in our classroom. You probably have a YouTube app on your phone at this moment to assist you in designing lessons that not only include reading and writing, but also speaking about the content! (See Appendix for an extended list.)

Remember the claps babies received for the attempts with language? Praising and acknowledging for the attempts of content language speaking is just as applicable in the content classroom. Validation is a strong confidence builder and language is an empowering tool! Students need to view themselves as successful content language users for them to continue with the language learning. Students will come to you with different levels of content language ability. We know that second language learners can withdraw from the learning process based on their experiences with using the language. If they have little or no confirmation from others that the effort was valued beyond paper and pencil assessment, self-confidence and a sense of belonging in that content language community will be low. On the other hand, if

---

AUTHENTIC SPEECHES (MENTOR AND STUDENT PRODUCED)

- Classroom peer and group
- Story telling/retelling
- Political/Activist role play
- Acceptance Award Speeches
- Actor/Singer Award Speeches
- Scholarship Awards
- Persuasive
- Activist Role Play
- Marketing/Sales
- Opinion
- Author Visit Role play
- Café-like casual discussion

they have encouragement for their acquisition attempts, they can develop a positive self-image of being a language learner (Cummings, 1994). Language learners learn best if they have a social content to make use of the way the language works. When offered group, peer, and individual opportunities to discuss in an academic but social setting, content language learners can make use of the new content knowledge and figure out how others use the language in such a setting. These social and linguistic processes provide schema building opportunities, which give value to learning the structure of the content language. If curiosity killed the cat, then assumption about students having effective content speaking skills simply because they can speak in their first language can damage the authentic language relationship. We can help our students build fluency for learning in the content areas by providing the examples and opportunities to speaking about the content.

Thinking. Center to reading, writing, speaking, and listening lays the thread that holds the five literacies together— thinking! In every part of acquiring content language, thinking is at the core. We cannot begin to learn a new content language without first thinking about what we already know and about what we want to learn. When reading, writing, and speaking, active learners are in a recurring cycle of pre-thinking, during-thinking, and after-thinking. This becomes easier when the content is self-selected as we are motivated by our personal curiosity to find out information. Does this change when the content is already decided for them? In most cases students do not get to choose what to learn about science, math, social studies, or other content language areas in the classroom setting. It is our job as content language teachers to help them develop this motivation for thinking by activating curiosity and asking them to wonder about what *within* an area of content needs to be uncovered. Personal goals for learning are crucial to successful language learning. As it was dangerous to assume that just because students can speak in their first language they can speak in the content language; it too is dangerous to assume that just because we are thinking creatures by nature that learners all come to the classroom knowing *HOW* and *WHAT* specifically to think about on a given topic. If you haven't yet noticed the pattern with these five literacies, on the content language teacher's side there must be structure, guidance, opportunity, and example for thinking like a person in that field of study.

What is meant by providing structure for thinking? Thinking goes beyond the simple question of what do you want to know or wonder about a given concept? Although that is a starting point, it only satisfies the "pre-thinking" part of the cycle process. To

BECOMING FLUENT IN THE LANGUAGE OF CONTENT

truly have content fluency, learners need to be able to continue that process into the "during and after" learning by explaining and manipulating the "facts" of content into their personal viewpoint for an authentic reason. Roberts and Billings (2008) explain that "teaching thinking has taught us that learning to think requires frequent, deliberate practice. To become clear, flexible, and coherent thinkers, students need to work with both the process and the product. The only way we have found to teach the process and product of thinking is to recognize the profound relationship between thought and language" (p. 32). As content language teachers, we need to deliberately plan for the active thinking process within our lessons before, during, and after our teaching. We need to structure what the students are thinking about and how that relates to previous thinking as well as current and future thinking.

No longer are the days that the teacher is the "talking head" of the classroom, rather the content language teacher must be the facilitator of the thinking process by offering structured opportunities to think about the content in relation to specific contexts. When we ask students to think about content we are asking them to *use* the content language on a very personal and fluent level. The opportunities we can provide for students for thinking frequently and deliberately help to validate, clarify, motivate, be predictive, and confirm factual knowledge learned about the content. This is the intersection of the five literacies for fluency in the language of content. As mentioned previously, this is not an assumed trait that comes with each student.

Guidance and example must be provided so students know just how a scientist, historian, and mathematician think about their content. With that said, it is important to point out that as you become a teacher, you also become a scientist, historian, and mathematician! You *are* an example of a thinker. The **think-aloud** is one of the best techniques available for teachers to open up the thinking process, to share and demonstrate the process. Through the process, teachers stop frequently during teaching to show students that they are an active thinker by modeling various thinking aspects. This is a one-way conversation between the content and the teacher, but as more demonstrations occur, the teacher will gradually release the thinking process to the students. Take a look at the "Authentic Think-Aloud Moments" box for some stem starters to model these conversations.

Listening. What does it mean to be an engaged listener? One very common assumption that can be made about learners is that they know how to be engaged as listeners. As with the other four literacies, using the literacy of listening requires one to first know what that means and how to use it.

AUTHENTIC THINKING OPPORTUNITIES

- How does this connect to what you previously knew about the content? (validation)
- What Ah-ha's have developed (clarifications)
- What Wow's have you uncovered (motivational and personal discoveries)
- What is "quote-worth" to share with another person (factual)
- How does this help to for new wonders about the text? (predictive)

Just merely listening is not necessarily something that needs to be taught, but being an engaged listener does! Too often learners are in environments that do not advocate for them to demonstrate that they are engaged with listening. These environments may expect learners to listen, but without means for the learner to demonstrate the task, they fall into a passive listener role, or possibly only engage with learning when called on to recall factual information. Even though this is a form of demonstrating listening, it is not demonstrating being an active and engaged listener. **Engaged listening** is when learners know they hold a responsibility to respond to learning by retelling what was spoken in a genuine conversational manner. This is slightly different than being engaged with the literacy of "speaking." As an engaged listener, students use eye contact and possibly may write down notes about what they heard, because they know there will be an opportunity to utilize the effort. This can be done between listener and teacher, listener and class, listener and listener, or listener and small group. During this opportunity, the listeners retell, paraphrase, or summarize what was presented or spoken to confirm their understanding and interpretation of the content using "listening" lingo such as those found in the Beginning Engaged Listener Stems box. This opportunity allows the learner to use the "language" in a confirming and affirming situation. When language learners are placed in opportunities that allow them to build ownership of the structure of the language by using it in an authentic context, content fluency is strengthened. Once again, content language teachers are going to model what it sounds like and looks like to be an engaged listener; but more importantly the modeling shows something even more valuable. It shows that you **are** an engaged listener.

WAYS CONTENT LANGUAGE TEACHERS CAN MODEL THE SPEAKING/LISTENING LITERACIES

While the Think-Aloud is a valuable technique for the teacher's toolbox, another tool that should be in all teachers toolbox is the Role Play-Example/Non-Example technique. This is a technique that allows the students to get involved with manipulating, confirming, and validating what you mean when you say 'engaged speaker and listener' (Please do not limit this just to these situations. Example/Non-example skits are GREAT classroom management techniques.) Using a skit-like platform, each participating student is provided a scenario to "act" out the literacy. One skit has the scenario for acting out what it means to be an active speaker/listener or the example scenario, and the other skit has the non-example or what it is not. This then allows the students to compare and contrast as well as connect to a visual meaning of what it means when a content language learner is engaged with the acquisition of learning the content language by listening and speaking. Keep the skits short but have several to use that are similar in nature so more students can participate and discussion (See appendix for more Example/Non-example scenarios.)

Example Scenario

Student 1: I just finished reading this great book on sharks. Did you know that their skin feels like sandpaper?

Student 2: No, I didn't. So I hear you say you read a book on sharks. What else did you find out?

Non-example Scenario

Student 1: I just finished reading this great book on sharks. Did you know that their skin feels like sandpaper?

Student 2: Yeah, I knew that.

Developing a Critical Eye for Lesson Design with the Five Literacies

Remember that classroom you thought about earlier where the Net-generation students use the social interaction of literacy to push learning outside the traditional boundaries? That will be your classroom, and those students will come to you needing their natural curiosity about the way the world works to be satisfied. The factual knowledge of content will no longer meet their needs. Even the youngest of learners can simply Google search or ask "Siri" to find it for them in the connected world in which they live. What they will need is someone to facilitate the acquisition of that content language and use it in fluent, meaningful, and authentic contexts. By using the five literacies as the intersecting and connecting element for content learning, learners become fluent in the way they read, write, speak, think, and listen about content. **Content fluency**, or the fluid and confident ability to use the language of the content in and out of formal and informal learning communities, is the goal for content language teachers!

Throughout this book, you will engage in a variety of strategies, activities, and approaches to build a teaching content language toolbox. The Content Language Lesson Design Checklist can help assist you with developing and designing lessons that develop content fluency through the five literacies. For example, in a given week of teaching, you will want to make sure that your lessons have one or more of each literacy embedded. The checklist will become a valuable resource for finding appropriate strategies to connect with the lesson at your fingertips. You will see that some strategies utilize just one type of literacy, while others might include all five. Given the time and goal of the lesson, you will become critical at which to use. A lesson that uses a strategy of more than three literacies gives that lesson more bang for the buck!

There will be many additional "content" purposes for strategies that help students become fluent in the content. Some will assist the learner with acquiring the language or vocabulary of the content. Others may help to organize knowledge or to assist with comprehension. And still others may be tools that can help learners develop/grant ownership for their opinions and learning. As with the five literacies, there can be more than one content purpose for the strategy—and the more purposes the better. Additionally, some strategies are considered **front loading** while others are **back loading** or best as a whole lesson. When a strategy helps to build and/or draw on schema before it is taught, that strategy is considered a frontloading type. If a strategy helps a learner to reflect or return to previous schema after a lesson or unit, this is considered a back loading type strategy. A lesson or unit of study can have both front and back loading strategies. As you come across strategies, use the checklist to value how useful it will be for you to guide your student toward becoming fluent in the language of content! Let's try one now!

Content Language Checklist

5 Literacies	Reading													
	Writing													
	Speaking													
	Thinking													
	Listening													
Learning Skill	Vocabulary													
	Content Comprehension													
	Content Organization													
	Content Ownership													
Type of Strategy	Front Loading													
	Back Loading													
	Whole Lesson													
Appropriate Level	Lower Elementary (PK-1)													
	Upper Elementary (2-6)													

POST-IT PREVIEW/REVIEW

Supplies: chart paper for a designated number of groups, colored markers/pens/crayons (one color per group AND one color per person in group), timer, and chime

Procedure for Post-It Preview:

1. Prior to class, create four to five open-ended questions related to the content topic that will be covered in the unit. These questions should NOT be quizzing in nature but rather open for sharing personal thoughts/experiences. For example, if a weather unit on hurricanes is about to begin, a possible question may be "What might you see outside during a very terrible storm?" Write one question on each of the pieces of chart paper at the top. Select your open-ended questions based on the content you wish to present. This will help guide you throughout the lesson/unit.

2. Divide the class into the number of questions and chart papers prepared. Give each group the same color marker/crayon and enough for each group member. This is to identify group responses.

3. Give a chart paper to each group. Instruct each member to silently read the question and to find a place anywhere on the chart paper to write a response. Give one minute to respond. Ring a chime to signal time over and have students share their responses for one minute. Rotate the chart paper to a new group going clockwise. The procedure will repeat until all questions have been addressed by all groups.

4. When the first chart paper has returned back to the original group, ask each group to read all the responses from other groups written on the paper. Have students summarize what generally was written by each colored group, and have each group share what was revealed about the class-wide opinion on the questions. Have them select a statement to "quote" that the group liked.

5. Indicate that these questions are related to the unit of study and purposefully post them in an area that can be easily referred back to throughout your teaching. When you teach/discuss about the content related to a specific question, reference some of the responses previously made.

6. This strategy can be used for after a lesson/unit of study as well.

STRATEGY ANALYSIS

From the back of this book, tear out a copy of the Lesson Design checklist. In the first slanted space at the top of the page, write in "Post-It Preview/Review." Now, let's work down the checklist. Reread the strategy and think about the five literacies it supports directly. How is this strategy helping learners use the content language that they will bring into the lesson, or that they have developed during the lesson? Are they engaged with meaningful reading experiences? Are they using the content language to communicate in written form, spoken form, to actively listen or think?

FIVE LITERACIES

- **Reading.** This strategy does have the learner reading other learners' posts, but this strategy does not assist them to actively navigate text for a reading purpose, so you would not check that box.
- **Writing.** When a learner communicates with others in an active written form using the language of the content, we can say that a strategy is using this form of literacy to assist the learner to develop content fluency. This box would be checked. In this situation, the learner was writing down personal responses related to the content and in doing so, had to use some content language.
- **Speaking.** When a learner is communicating with others in an active, spoken form using the language of the content, we can say that a strategy is using this form of literacy to assist the content fluency. This box would be checked. In this situation there were many speaking opportunities to use content language. After the initial post, learners shared their personal post with the group, then after all groups had the time to respond to the question, the group discussed together what similar and different posts were written, they spoke among each other to consolidate and summarize posts, and then presented this information to the class.
- **Thinking.** When a learner is offered the opportunity to actively formulate thoughts using the language of content, we can say that a strategy is supporting the "thinking" aspect of literacy. This box would be checked. In this situation there were many thinking opportunities to formulate their personal response about the content. This can be seen in the initial post and especially in the group analysis of all the posts.
- **Listening.** This strategy does have the learner listening to other group members' sharing of their posts but does not assist the learner to actively engage in response to listening so you would not check that box.

LEARNING SKILL

- **Vocabulary.** When a learner is offered the opportunity to develop new vocabulary or language of the content, we can say that the strategy is supporting the learner to acquire more of the content language. This strategy did not support vocabulary or language development so you will not check this box.

- **Content comprehension**. When a learner is offered the opportunity to demonstrate content comprehension/understanding, we can say that the strategy is supporting the learner to use that knowledge to make a connection to learning. This strategy allowed for the learner to demonstrate prior knowledge of the content in order to make connection to future learning experiences so you will check this box.

- **Content organization.** When a learner is offered the opportunity to specifically organize content with a form of graphic organization or other ordering design, we can say that the strategy is supporting the learning to manage the content being learned. This strategy did not support content organization.

- **Content ownership.** When a learner is offered the opportunity to take ownership of content known or learned, we can say that the strategy is supporting the learner to own the learning experience. This strategy allowed the learner to own his or her knowledge or experience by sharing, presenting, validating, contradicting, adapting, and connecting to content using the language of the content You will check this box.

TYPE OF STRATEGY

This strategy is designed to be a front loading strategy as it is being done before teaching has begun. How could this be designed to be a back loading strategy?

APPROPRIATE LEVEL

This strategy would best be suited for grades 2–6 due to the written and analytic nature of the strategy, but how could this be tiered down to be used in kindergarten or first grade?

Something to Think About!

As the content language teacher, you will want to form a very critical eye for designing lessons. How will the lessons help your students move beyond acquiring facts and toward becoming fluent in the language of content? You will need to think about the unit of study with the intent of providing multiple opportunities to socially connect with the content using the five literacies. It will require thoughtful consideration of the strategies you select to complement the knowledge being taught. It will require you to move beyond the act of teaching facts, and toward the art of guiding your students to becoming fluent in the language of your content!

What is reading but silent conversation?
– Walter Savage Landor

Chapter Two

Strategies to Support Engaged Learning through the Five Literacies

However beautiful the strategy, you should occasionally look at the results. --Winston Churchill

In our previous chapter, you were introduced to the framework for helping students become fluent in the language of content through the intentional exposure of the five literacies: reading, writing, thinking, speaking, and listening. With this framework, a foundation has been set for how critically you will view designing content lessons. As a content language teacher, you are moving past the mere exposure of facts and toward assisting students to become fluent users of the content language. Now, let's get strategic!

Strategy. To help you connect to this term, think about a sports-related competitive event. The two teams are neck-and-neck to win the game; the one coach devises a **strategy**, which will have the players divert the attention of the other team so that his team can be successful. Teachers use strategies when teaching to assist students with successful learning. In competitive situations, strategies are purposely kept secret for the element of surprise. Okay, spoiler alert! … There is NO secret to the strategies teachers use! And yet, too often they are kept hidden for teachers' eyes only.   It is imperative that you let your learners know "THIS IS A STRATEGY called "XYZ," which YOU TOO can use when learning!" Too often teachers overlook to explicitly name the teaching strategy and address it as a usable "student strategy." The strategies presented in this book will definitely make for engaged lessons to aid building content fluency. However, if we hold this knowledge of strategic learning to ourselves, we lose an opportunity for students to carry the strategy over to their independent learning. For students to build content fluency, they will need to know how to use "named" strategies, which will assist them in diverse learning settings beyond the classroom walls. With that said, have you ever heard of the saying that it takes 6 to 10 times for something to become a habit? That is the same in the classroom. Content language teachers will need to explicitly and routinely expose students to content language strategies embedded in lessons before independent use can be expected. The approach you will take with students must encourage the learner to utilize the same strategy on additional occasions. While variety has its place in lesson design, it is not necessary for a new and improved strategy to be created for every lesson. In this case, repetition is good. The more comfortable students become with strategies embedded in your lessons, the more likely transfer of that to independent learning can take place. This chapter will present in-depth approaches for using strategies within content lessons related to building content fluency through the five literacies. The strategy types that will be introduced are front loading and back loading strategies for developing schema and content language acquisition.

Teacher-led Strategy → Student participation → Explicit Naming by teacher → Repeated exposure → Student Independence and Content Fluency

Front Loading and Back Loading

Although we are naturally curious about the world around us and are social creatures with the need to find ways to communicate, we are also wired to make meaning out of that curiosity and social interaction. Humans function on the premise of making connections to make meaning. We continuously reflect on experiences based on what prior knowledge exists related to the new experience and how best to move forward. This self-reflection forces us to decide if we know something about the topic and if that "something" is a high level of knowledge or low level. In doing so, we metaphorically open up filing cabinets in our minds to see where a new knowledge set can be filed or make determinations about the need for a new file to be created. This is a most fortunate set of skills for us as well as for a content language teacher. The level of knowledge can be used as a motivational tool for learning if we tap into it! Strategies that front load a learning experience are quite powerful for a teacher. They have the potential of validating learners' prior knowledge, establishing what curiosities still exist about the learning, building motivation, and allowing for communications opportunities to be shared about these wonders.

Front loading is a type of strategy that allows the content language teacher to set up these experiences ahead of the learning through interactive activities. It is more than just asking what they know about the topic, it is literally "loading up" the learning experiences before teaching even begins. Let's take a simple example that you can relate to, such as your first day of grade school. Imagine that August has arrived and you begin the steps of preparing for the experience of the first day of school. You go clothes shopping and supply shopping, you pick the just-right backpack and lunch box, and you may even make contact with friends who are coming back from summer vacations. All of these tasks are preparing you AND motivating you for the first day of school. You are excited, curious, and can't wait to socially exchange these wonders with classmates. This is the exact experience that front loading does for content units of study. As a teacher, this will be your plan of action for establishing interest and motivation for **engaged learning**. Take a look at the sidebar "Front Loading Activities." Notice that taking a field trip or showing a movie is listed with these activities. Many times these might be considered the culminating activity or the "reward" for the unit taught. In front loading, this starts the process rather than finishes it. Can't make it off campus? Take a virtual Google image exploration voyage as well as a Google search! Set the search engine to "image" and provide some preselected guide terms for a search. This is especially useful when dealing with historical units to set a visual image about the content language they will be acquiring. Implementing these at the front of a unit allows you to use the experience as a springboard for your lessons! Front loading activities are considered longer than the typical "activating prior knowledge" activity. There is usually a large amount of time set aside at the beginning of a learning unit to "load-up" and build motivation for learning. Some may even take all the allotted time. With this understanding of front loading, back loading can be assumed as the opposite, where knowledge gained during learning experiences is validated and valued. Back loading is something more often used by teachers even if the term is not. It can be considered the culminating aspect of a unit of study or of a lesson within the unit of study. On a large scale, back loading can be the connecting field trip, media presentation, guest presenter, or student project. On the small scale, it can be the closing element or returning to a front loading strategy for a daily lesson or at the end of a week. All of the suggestions from "Frontloading Activities" can also be back loading.

Before we develop the concept of front loading further, we need to return to the focus of helping our students become fluent in the language of content by using the language in authentic situations. The way the previously mentioned activities are presented can seem passive and even teacher-centered if not extended to include aspects of the five literacies. Students should be

---

FRONT LOADING ACTIVITIES

- Field trips
- Movie/documentary premiere
- Virtual Google Image exploration
- Google searches
- Power Pictures Murals
- Puzzler
- Unlock the Door
- Guest Speaker

Let's add this to the Content Language Acquisition Framework chart! What can you check off for its active engagement in building content fluency?

THINK-PAIR-SHARE

1. Teacher begins by suggesting a topic, asking a question, or viewing/ listening to media.
2. Students "think" and write down their opinions, thoughts, connections, and/or wonders related to the tasks.
3. Students "pair" up with another student and "share" what was written.
4. Whole class discussion about what was shared. It is good to give permission to share something that was either shared personally or what was heard by a classmate. Many times students do not mind sharing with one student but have reservations with the whole class. One way to still grant ownership to their opinion is for their partner or group members to share with the class what was "heard."

Adapted from *Project CRISS: Creating Independence through Student-owned Strategies.* (Santa, Havens, & Maycumber, 1996, p. 34)

actively thinking and speaking about the content read, written, or heard—and in some cases viewed on a daily basis. Rich conversations can be the link to building motivation and for owning learning experiences but they do not happen by chance. Effective teachers plan for them. One effective strategy for developing a rich conversation environment in your classroom is with **Think-Pair-Share**. This strategy allows for natural and structured conversation. While it is discussed here in the front loading section, this is a tactic that can be used with diverse learning situations. The beauty about Think-Pair-Share is that it levels the playing field for all to have an opportunity to voice their opinions, thoughts, and wonders by offering the time to organize these in written form, then share them in a low-risk environment. It is important to point out that every time students are asked to voice their opinion (be it whole class or small group), they are taking a risk. We need to respect and value that risk by providing opportunities for them to cash in on the investment they made in the learning experience. Such situations create student ownership of the content language learning process.

Valuing and Validating Learning. Prior to the 1980s, valuing what students brought to the learning experiences as well as their natural curiosities was not regularly used in classroom teaching. During the 1980s, researchers began making strong correlations to positive learning outcomes when teachers tapped into the schema or prior knowledge of students. In 1986, one of the most commonly used terms today, K-W-L, was introduced to teachers by Donna Ogle. She created this model to help teachers utilize the knowledge students already had about a concept and followed that with inquiry and validation measures. The three simple components of the model ask "What do you KNOW?" then "What do you WANT to know?" and "What did you LEARN?" prior to engaging in a new learning experience (Ogle, 1986). Ogle found that when using the model, students felt they had a part in the learning process and teachers had the opportunity to value the students' prior knowledge and curiosity by designing more effective individualized content lessons. The KWL model falls into the front loading category as it sets up the stage for learning. There are many ways to utilize this model, but the most common is the three-column graphic organizer, which is either whole class completed or individually done by students. It is easy to see why this model became successful as it opened up dialogue between teacher and student as well as between student and student. The basic procedures for the KWL are:

- Begin by asking students what they already **know** about the topic of study. The teacher may have the chart written on a large chart paper and solicits responses from the whole class. These responses are recorded in the first column, K.
- Next, solicit curiosities regarding **what** the class would like to learn about the topic or more currently what they **wonder** about. These responses are recorded in the second column, W.
- Finally, as a back loading strategy, solicit for factual knowledge **learned** from the learning experience at the end of a learning experience. These responses are recorded in the third column, L. This should happen on a regular basis at the end of a day's lesson, at the end of a week's learning, and at the end of a unit taught.

When we ask students to take a risk and participate in determining the direction for their learning, a more engaged learning environment is created. Students become more emotionally involved with their learning and motivated to participate when they are asked to be part of the process. Additionally when they see that you have a personal interest in what they know and want to know about the learning process, students take a more active role in learning (VanDeWeghe, 2009). The **KWL** model, as you have probably experienced yourself, has many aspects to the five literacy framework we are using to build content fluency. It is a tried and true approach to creating meaningful and individualized learning experiences for your students whether you chose to use this as a whole class or as an individual graphic organizing learning tool, below are just a few things to think about.

TIPS:

- For time efficiency the teacher should be the scribe for whole class recording.
- When doing this as a whole class activity, put the student initials by the response written down to give ownership to that comment or thought.
- Refer back **often** to the knowledge known, questions stated, and new knowledge learning. Use the students' initials to give validations to the investment made at the beginning of the learning process. As lessons are progressing, check off questions answered in the W column. Add new information to the L column which answers the questions. You may even find that students develop more questions as the teaching evolves!
- If time runs out for you to return **often** to the L column of the model as a back loading strategy, you can use the model as an "introduction/review" for the next day's lessons and begin by adding any new information learned thus far.
- IMPORTANT: Never leave a question in the W column unanswered! At the end of a teaching unit, if there is still something left in the W column, assign this as an "Expert Researcher/Scholar Challenge." Write the question on an index card and ask for a volunteer to become the expert on this question and report it back to the class on a given day. Make this an important role. Get a graduation "cap and gown" and as a "scholar" let the students wear this on the day they present the information learned about the question. You will have students begging to take on this role! This also shows to the class that while it might not have been answered during the teaching process, it was a valuable question that still needs to be investigated. If this is not done, there runs the risk that whoever asked that question may feel his or her contribution to the pre-learning experience was undervalued and possibly withdraw from the KWL experience next time.

Evolving the KWL model. The KWL model is a wonderful front loading strategy. The truth is, while whole class use of the KWL model has its advantages it also has limitations. To better understand this, visualize using the KWL model in a classroom with 20 students. Do you have the image? Describe to yourself what is happening in the classroom AND what is not happening. Did you envision all 20 students raising their hand, waiting patiently for you to write each response down in each column for each student? We have talked about the advantages to tapping into students' prior knowledge using the KWL, but in reality for you to ensure that all 20 students are actively engaged in the KWL model will take more than half the allotted teaching time as well as half your class becoming off task and disengaged after the first 10 minutes. So, you might think about calling on selected students to represent the class. Well, if only selected volunteers contribute, whole class engagement suffers. Students may internally be thinking about what they know and what they want to find out, but they fear the risk to openly share their opinions and wonders are left out as a consequence. Time constraints may limit who gets called on and who doesn't. Remember, strategies must be modeled multiple times (no matter how many years they have been exposed to it) before *you* can simply hand them the graphic organizer to complete on their own. Although that would help with time efficiency, the time to involve, model, and demonstrate its use becomes a concern as well. So, what is to be done?

The basic components of the KWL are vital pieces for fostering engaged learning opportunities and you are encouraged to utilize the components when designing lessons. The following two front loading activities, Puzzler and Unlock the Door, evolve the traditional KWL experience by creating low-risk and time-efficient opportunities for all students to become engaged learners in the process of building content fluency through the five literacies. These strategies complement each other well, but can also be done in isolation.

Unlock the Door Strategies

MATERIALS:

1 Large chart paper size *keyhole* with "Unlock the Door to…"
4–5 colored pieces of paper
4–5 concept terms
Copy of the blackline "key" sheet (1 per student)

Puzzler. In some circumstances, students might think they have limited prior knowledge to a content topic if asked in too general of a question such as, "What do you know about volcanoes?" They also might not be willing to share their knowledge to the whole class, but would be willing to take that risk in a smaller group of students. To give them structure to the pre-thinking process, break down the topic into four to five concept terms that you intend to explore during your unit of study such as "magma," "lava," "ring of fire," "dormant," and "Hawaii." This usually works well to think of the amount of terms based on the ratio to groups you can divide the class into. Below are the steps for continuing the strategy for engaging students in discussion about the prior knowledge they may have about the topic.

UNLOCK THE DOOR TO…

Let's add this to the Content Language Acquisition Framework chart! What can you check off for its active engagement in building content fluency?

PROCEDURES:

1. Write/type one concept onto each sheet of colored paper in large font using a different color for each concept to create the puzzler cards. Group students into four or five groups with no more than four or five students in each group. For example, magma, lava, ring of fire, dormant, and Hawaii. TIP: For kindergarten and first grade, select pictures from textbooks or the internet that visualize the meaning of the concept.

Example of Concept Puzzler cards

 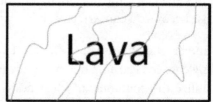

2. Cut each piece of paper into four to five simple "puzzle" pieces. For each colored paper, vary the puzzle design. The total amount of all puzzle pieces should equal one per student. See example of Concept Puzzle cards.
3. Copy the blackline master "key" sheet (Appendix) so that there is a key for each student.
4. Shuffle all puzzle pieces and pass out one to each student along with one key.
5. Instruct students that they will do the following:
    *   Find the other classmates with the same color puzzle piece.
    *   Find a desk/table to put the puzzle together.
    *   As a group, read the word/concept that is on the puzzle.
    *   Independently, each student will then list on the back of the key all that they know about the concept from the puzzle piece.
    *   Independently, each student will write one question on the front of the inside of the key. They may put their name on it if they like.
    *   Allow time for each member of the group to share what they know and wonder about.

Sample Key Card for Unlock the Door

- Select a "spokesperson" for the group, and have each group present to the class a summary of what the group knows about the concept and what they want to know about the concept from the key cards.

6. Post the "Unlock the Door" chart poster in an area that you can leave the chart over the course of the unit study. For example, "Unlock the Door to . . . learning about Volcanoes."

7. As the student presents the questions from the group, use double-sided tape or ticky-tac to place the "key" question card around the outside of the keyhole on the "Unlock the Door" poster. (Combine/staple similar questions together.)

8. During the course of your lessons, return often to the "Unlock the Door" poster as a back loading strategy and read questions on the key cards. Ask the students if that question has been answered. If it has, have the class discuss what they now know about the answer to the question, then remove the key from the outside of the keyhole and place it inside the keyhole. They are now beginning to "Unlock the Door to learning more about volcanoes." The goal will be to move all the question cards into the keyhole to completely unlock the mystery to this concept.

9. Any question keys not answered by the end of the unit of study should be used as the "Research/Scholar Challenge" as stated previously.

10. If only using the Puzzler activity, back load this activity by passing out the puzzle pieces again at the end of the lesson or unit of study following the same procedures. Allow for students to now validate new knowledge gained about the concepts.

At this point, students have now shared what they "know" about the concept, discussed what they "wonder" in relation to the topic, and periodically have validated new knowledge learned by moving the key card into the keyhole. These activities set up the students predicted learning experiences to align with your lesson designs, because you selected concepts based on what will be taught. Unlock the Door keeps the KWL active and alive in your classroom by creating a student-centered environment. All students participate in this frontloading activity, allowing them to become engaged and motivated to find out more to unlock the door. What is powerful about these strategies is the visual acknowledgement of the actual learning process. Prior to your teaching, there is a visual representation of what is *not* known about the topic. At the completion of your lessons, students can actually see the "learning process" from the keys that have been moved into the keyhole. "Unlock the Door" activity can be used alone, but by adding the puzzler the strategy builds vocabulary and language structure for creating opportunities to speak the content in an appropriate context. When you do these activities, step back and watch how **engaged** your students are at becoming fluent speakers, listeners, and thinkers of the content being studied before you even begin!

Engaged Learning and Front Loading. At this point you have a good idea of the impact front loading strategies can have on helping your students become fluent in the language of content by tapping into the five literacies. Much like society has developed a hunger for multifunctional and engaged lifestyles, so too has education as it moves into the 21st century and the need to engage students in meaningful learning has evolved. While student engagement has been a perpetual outcome for education, how it is perceived has more recently included characteristics of a changing society that relies on a social atmosphere to connect to learning. Think about ways you socially interact to create meaning of something or to extend your opinion on an issue. How many different modes of "language" are you utilizing to make yourself heard? Can you begin to see how content language acquisition and the strategies being presented will help your students use language to be heard in the context of your classroom?

For past decades, engaged learning has been viewed as the observable behaviors during involvement with an educational activity. This has generally been assessed by observing the behaviors of the learner. Multiple aspects of observing **behavioral** **engagement** can be attributed to either active (positive) or inactive (negative) engagement such as attendance, participation, completion of tasks, and directions followed (VanDeWeghe, 2006). But can we really say a student was engaged in learning because he or she completed an assignment or was quiet while a teacher was lecturing on a topic? More recently, educators have urged for an expanded explanation for engaged learning to include emotional and cognitive engagement in learning as it has been found that students obtain a richer learning experience when these areas of learning are addressed (Harcourt & Keen, 2012). **Emotional** **engagement** can be explained by connections the learner makes with the educational activity. This includes the level of interest or value for the learning situation including feelings and values toward the teacher, peers, and environment. Engagement in learning can be both positively and negatively affected by the emotional engagement for learning. **Cognitive** **engagement** involves the level of thoughtful commitment to the learning activity the student puts forth. This can be connected to the level of critical thinking and the challenge that is posed by the educational activity. For example, lecture-like activities provide a low level of cognitive learner engagement, whereas student discovery groups embedded with discussion opportunities offer a highly cognitive engagement.

Engaged learning theory involves many factors to address the behavioral, emotional, and cognitive needs of students. VanDeWeghe (2006) explains that classroom factors such as teacher–student and student–peer relationship, teacher support and design for engaged learning opportunities, and the students' individual needs must be included for nurturing optimal environments for student engagement with learning.

Theory holds that engagement in learning will be enhanced in classrooms where the tasks (a) are authentic, (b) provide opportunities for students to assume ownership of their conception, execution, and evaluation; (c) provide opportunities for collaboration; (d) permit diverse forms of talents; and (e) provide opportunities for "fun" (p. 91).

This "flow" of engagement offers a holistic environment where students feel a sense of belonging, autonomy, and competency in their learning outcomes. When such a state of engagement is achieved, it offers successful opportunities for student learning (Shernoff et al., 2003). Let's investigate another strategy that allows for students to assume ownership, validate their preconceived opinions for learning, collaborate with peers, and oh, yea… have fun!

Anticipation Guides. Similar to the previous front loading activities discussed, the Anticipation Guide is another approach you can use to set the stage and motivate students for future learning. When teachers activate prior knowledge with students, they are tapping into what students "think" they know about a particular topic. Sometimes this is accurate; sometimes they have been misguided in their understanding; and sometimes there is no prior knowledge to draw from requiring an educated guess to be risked. Learning opportunities occur not just when learners realize something new has been added to their knowledge base, but also when prior knowledge has been confirmed *and* even contradicted. Anticipation Guides are tools teachers can use to help students validate and assume ownership for the learning experience. Traditional Anticipation Guides are paper-based and provide individual learners the opportunity to state an opinion about content to be learned prior to engaging in a unit of study. The teacher creates several statements drawn from the lesson and formats these statements into a chart-like presentation so learners can "agree" or "disagree" with the statement based on their prior knowledge. This requires student investment and a level of risk taking to gamble on their opinions about what they know. Many times, a statement is too difficult to make such a one-sided opinion and in these situations placing a check between the two is perfectly acceptable. The teacher will back load the learning experience by returning to the Anticipation Guide, allowing for students to validate original opinions or change them based on new knowledge gained.

Now, what we know about engaged learning is that it should offer a learner the opportunity to participate in a learning activity (behavioral), own their learning through a form of communication (cognitive), and have some fun with the learning experience (emotional). Providing a paper-based Anticipation Guide is an individual activity that does engage a learner behaviorally and cognitively, but it is lacking in the emotional engagement arena. What emotions can you engage by passing out a sheet of paper to a student? How much happiness to explore a new topic will this engagement create for them? The amount of that engagement is a bit too limited to make that assumption.

AGREE	DISAGREE	STATEMENT
		Lava is the only thing that comes out of an erupting volcano.
		Hawaii is located on a hot spot.
		The ring of fire is something a circus animal jumps through.
		Lava can be a good soil for plants to grow in.
		A volcanologist is a person from another planet called Vulcan.
		Magma is lava before it erupts from a volcano.
		All mountains are volcanoes

Traditional Anticipation Guide

Let's add this to the Content Language Acquisition Framework chart! What can you check off for its active engagement in building content fluency?

Some wisdom or advice is appropriate at this moment (in addition to the pages and pages you are getting from this book) … any paper-pencil activity can be made into an engaging opportunity that meets the description above. By designing *out* of the activity the paper and then putting *into* an activity the opportunity for learners to use multiple literacies for learning, a teacher creates a socialized and collaborative environment rich for developing behavioral, emotional, and cognitive engagement. Let's look at the Agree and Disagree activity modified for creating a flow of engagement for learning.

Agree/Disagree Strategy (Modification of an Anticipation Guide)

MATERIALS:

2 card stock sheets of paper per group of 3–4 students
1 set of 8–10 content statements (one statement on a slip of paper)
1 envelope

One set of 3–4 "demo" statement cards for modeling

1. Fold the cardstock paper in half so that each creates a "tent" to set on a tabletop.
2. On one tent, write "agree" on both sides. For the other tent, write "disagree" on both sides.
3. Use large enough font to print out your content statements on regular paper so that each can be cut into strips. Place all strips in an envelope.
4. Create a demonstration set of 3–4 statement cards that are not related to the content for modeling.
5. Divide the class into groups of 3–4 students. Give each group a set of tent cards and one set of statements in an envelope.

6. Set the tents on opposite sides of the desks.
7. Once the students are in their groups, model for the students how to agree and disagree properly with the "demo" statements. The procedures are:
   - Take out a slip of paper and read aloud the statement placing it in the middle of the two tents.
   - Privately decide if you agree with the statement or disagree. (Teacher does a Think Aloud about the thinking process for making a decision.)
   - Allow for each student to share his or her opinion, providing a reason for why you think that way.
   - Place the statement under the appropriate tent.
   - Continue until all slips are read and decided on.
8. Have the students keep the tents and slips together, by placing the slips inside the folded tent and setting aside.
9. Proceed with the content lesson.
10. Back load the lesson by having the students revisit the Agree and Disagree tents and the slips they separated during front loading. As a group they will validate and confirm if the statements are still in the correct tent. If any statements are moved, an explanation for the move should be given.
11. Close the lesson by presenting the correct categories for the statements to the class. Have the groups discuss what was new information, what was challenged information (an opinion changed), and what was validated information.

Either the traditional or modified version of Anticipation Guides are great strategies for students to become self-aware of their preconceptions, form realization of new information gained, challenge opinions, and validate information known. Although this tool is used to visually and actively state, validate, build, and contradict new and learned knowledge, if modeled and demonstrated properly, Anticipation Guides help learners to practice the "act" of **metacognatively** becoming aware of these moments of learning. By gradually releasing control of using these tools, learners begin to see the act of stating opinions and challenging them for validation and contradiction aspects as a natural flow for engagement in the learning process. Having this as an internal strategy allows learners to have a critical skill available to them for future learning both in and out of school.

A Flow of Engagement for Content Language Acquisition. Flow theory in regard to engaged learning can be described as the intricate and transactional relationship the learner has with a learning experience. Csikszentmihalyi (1990) explains flow theory to be "when people seem driven to learn by some compelling force, when they find themselves totally enveloped in an exhilarating search for knowledge, answers, insight, or accomplishment, they are likely to encounter states of optimal experience that are intellectual, emotional, physical, spiritual, or any combination thereof" (p. 1). In flow theory, once students become emotionally and cognitively engaged, they begin to pose thoughts and questions that challenge their personal learning goals. They seek out to resolve the questions and thoughts but also continue to pose more until the learning challenge has been met, creating a deep bond with the

The flow of Engaged Learning to support content language acquisition

learning situation. Outside of the classroom, think of a performance arts individual mastering the delivery of a selected role in a play. This person becomes vested in rising to the challenge, seeking out approaches to perfect the task, and waiting for validation of his or her effort by more experienced individuals. It is through this transactional stage that the flow between the "states" of engagement can be recognized, the behavioral traits observed, and enjoyment in learning achieved. A learner develops "concentration" for the objective, "interest" for the topic, and "enjoyment" of the pursuit to meet the challenge. Can you think of a time when you were in a "flow" of learning something? What did it look and feel like to be in a successful learning experience? Think about the Unlock the Door Strategy, the Puzzler, or Agree/Disagree. How do these front loading strategies help the student move into a flow of engaged learning environment?

A grounding piece to the flow of engagement is the reinforcement factor (Shernoff et al., 2003). For flow between the states to be symbiotic, immediate teacher feedback is of high value to the learner as this keeps the learner on the correct path to achieving the learning outcome. This concept of teacher acknowledgement was presented briefly in chapter 1 when introducing the five literacies. Without positive feedback the cycle of engagement halts as the learner has no clear direction toward the outcome (Shernoff et al., 2003, 160-161). Classroom application of flow theory cannot be incidentally sought after; it must be a state of mind for educators to embrace if students are to be moved toward a "critical" level of engagement. There is a strong effort required by the teacher to seek out student interests and address personal character traits as well as become emotionally involved with the classroom dynamics between environment, teacher, and student. As a teacher, you must purposely create the environments that will best foster engagement with learning. We are helping students engaged with learning when we view teaching content as learning a new language to become fluent readers, writers, thinkers, speakers, and listeners of the content. Let's now explore how front loading strategies, which develop the "language" or vocabulary of content, provide such engaging opportunities!

Building Content Language Structure: a.k.a. Vocabulary

Our premise for teaching content has been one that allows the student to become fluent in the language of content. For content fluency to develop there needs to be a purpose for using and acquiring the language. We argue that literacy, language acquisition skills, fluency, and community must work together for students to add the language of content to their first language repertoire. Your classroom community environment must provide the need to *use* the language of content in authentic experiences. Think about this for a moment. When learning a second language, being immersed in that language and having the opportunity for practicing the language structure of vocabulary in a proper context sets students up to acquire that language. The term "use it or lose it" applies to this situation. Vocabulary of a language structure is needed for the student to build fluency. Over the years, vocabulary development took on a one-sided approach of merely learning the meaning of terms to know the content. Durham, Ingram, and Contreas-Vanegas (2014) discussed that second language acquisition (SLA) is when someone is beginning to learn another language after already having acquired a first one. More specifically, SLA is when someone learns another language after the early years of childhood. Additionally, students acquire a language when being exposed to examples of the language and its proper uses. Learners of a new language require more effective strategies than vocabulary lessons of meaning memorization. They need to embrace the purpose of using the terms in its content language context. The conversational interaction is vital for language learners to experiment with placing the need to use the term in an appropriate authentic situation.

Frontloading to Build Language Structure. The days when teachers sent home a list of words for students to find the "dictionary" meaning, use in sentences, and memorize for tests are just not meaningful enough for 21st-century learners. The age of hyperlinked words within digital readings or instant access to online dictionaries, make that aspect of teaching nearly as prehistoric as dinosaurs. Authentic and conversation-based language building activities will offer more advantages for students to become content fluent. Now, you just need to have a critical eye for selecting **concepts** and related terms to support the building extending schema for students. Front loading language structure activities continue to build on students' engagement with the pre-learning experiences. Let's explore some strategies that will provide opportunities for students to test their preconceived understanding of concepts and validate or contradict those understanding to build and extend schema and language use of the concepts.

I Think! I Know!

MATERIALS:

Multicolored beach ball
Vis-a-Vis pen
Selected concepts

PROCEDURE:

1. Select five concept/vocabulary words from the selected unit of study that students may not know or have difficulty with them. Write them on each color of the beach ball.
2. Introduce the ball and the words written on each color. Explain that these may be new and unfamiliar, but that the object of the activity is to "predict" what they **think** the word means.
3. Toss the ball to a student. The student will guess a meaning for the word that their left thumb landed on. They do not have to be correct. This is just a guess. It is very important for the student to use the language "I think" or "I know" what the term means.
4. The student with the ball tosses it back to the teacher and the procedure is repeated. If a word that has already been said is chosen, they can either say the same meaning (agree with someone else—but they must repeat the meaning, "I agree with Student A that 'I think' it means ...") or give a new one.
5. At the end of the activity, go back over the words repeating what some people said they might mean. You will not "provide" the meaning, but rather let the students draw the conclusion about if their preconceived understanding was validated, or if it was modified throughout the lessons. Instruct the class to listen carefully to the reading or lesson for the day or during the week. They will need to verify if what they thought it meant was correct, or if they need to make a change.

6. Repeat this activity after each session to check if new meanings are given. The goal is to have the students change or validate meaning, and by the end of the unit all words should be known with the correct context and agreed upon definition.

There are several unique elements to "I think, I know" that are empowering for students. It allows students to take a low risk for stating their thoughts knowing that it doesn't need to be correct on day 1. The strategy also creates multiple authentic experiences to use content language structure in acceptable language situations. Students state what their opinion is about the concepts in their own language using schema to form their opinion. Likewise, throughout the unit of study, they are reformulating those opinions out of the new knowledge gained validating, extending, or contradicting as each lesson progresses. As a teacher, you are not giving a predefined meaning for the concept, but rather letting the learning experiences you designed shape that meaning for them using the context of their schema. As you regularly engage the student before and after lessons with "I think, I know," you will begin to hear an empowering voice develop. In a given school week, on Monday you may hear the majority of your students say "I think this word means…" in a cautious and uncertain manner. By Wednesday, the class will begin to shift its tone and a more confident voice will be heard saying, "I know this word/term means… ." By Friday, the majority if not all of your class will confidently own the understanding of the terms by saying, "I know this word/term means… ." Vola! Without instructing to memorize a predetermined word list in isolation, "I think, I know" allows students to use the concepts in a spoken context and to form their own meaning that makes sense to them. You have embedded several new content language concepts to the students working language vocabulary where they are becoming authentic and fluent speakers, listeners, and thinkers of that content language. To hear students own that learning is, in return, empowering for the teacher!

BALANCING THE CONCEPTS

-   Determine students' level of prior knowledge with the concepts and terms.
-   Determine important concepts and specialized terms. Think of words that relate and support each other to develop the larger concept of the lessons.
-   Be efficient with your time and the students by selecting concepts that will benefit content fluency.
-   It is a balancing act between what is needed for the unit of study and the prior knowledge of the students.

Adopted from Allan & Miller (2005). *Literacy and Learning in the Content Areas: Strategies for Middle and Secondary Teachers.* pp. 104-109.

TIPS:

-   Plan for very excited students the first few times using the beach ball.
-   When beginning this strategy, toss the ball from teacher to student and back to teacher. As the students demonstrate acceptable and trustworthy engagement with the strategy, they can begin to toss the ball from student to student.
-   Set expectations for the strategy. Let the students know what it should look like to toss the ball from student back to teacher. Model this with a

student. Also set expectations for what it should not look like by modeling with a student.

- Write each term on popsicle sticks rather than a beach ball and use a cup to pass around from student to student.
- Modify for kindergarten students with pictures to represent the longer and more challenging terms. By the end of the week, they will begin to have "sight" word recognition for the terms that might be levels above their reading ability, but it will be in their speaking vocabulary!

Modifying for kindergarten and first grade

Visual Concept Language Maps

The following language building activity is designed to help students make connections to their prior understanding of the concept as well as to build their own understanding with new information. It serves as a visual organizer of content to develop language of a concept as students are engaged in conversation.

MATERIALS

white paper, colors

PROCEDURES:

1. Prior to the unit of study, decide on a theme/concept for students to visually depict in drawing. All students can have the same theme/concept, or you can divide themes into groups of students.
2. Preselect 4–5 identifiable language vocabulary concepts to develop.
3. Allow students to visually represent the theme by illustrating everything they know about the topic.
   - Ask students to use multiple colors.
   - Ask students to include the whole page.
   - Ask students to continue drawing until time is called. This may mean adding more detail if done earlier than time.
4. Ask students to "shoulder whisper" with a student in their group about everything they illustrated in their picture. Students may add information if they hear their partner mentioning things that are not in their drawing.
5. After the lessons and as a back loading activity, refer back to the drawing. Introduce one of the preselected vocabulary words at a time. Have students identify each vocabulary word and LABEL it on their drawing. If that aspect is not in the illustration, have them find a way to include it into the picture.
6. As lessons on the topic are taught, revisit the visual concept language map and add LABELS for new information.
7. Ask students to "shoulder whisper" with a student in their group about everything they added to the illustration. Students may add information if they hear their partner mentioning things that are not in their drawing.

With Visual Concept Language mapping, the visual concept map becomes a study/review tool. Because the students began with their own knowledge of the concept, they were able to visually validate that knowledge and then build on that with the new knowledge learned as they engaged in the learning process behaviorally, emotionally, and cognitively. Look at the example of a Visual Concept map where the teacher wanted to extend the knowledge of ecosystems, community, population, and habitat. Compare the "before and after" illustrations and think about how engaged the students were with the content language process.

> Let's add this to the Content Language Acquisition Framework chart! What can you check off for its active engagement in building content fluency?

4th grade Jocelynn's Visual Concept Language Map—Before lesson

4th grade Jocelynn's Visual Concept Language Map—After lesson

Something to Think About!

Connecting to Vygotsky's theory, content language development is the result of social interactions with the five literacies. Learning occurs when a person interacts with others on his or her zone of proximal development (ZPD). As content language teachers, using front loading and back loading strategies allows for students to have a purpose for tapping into their prior knowledge as a tool, and using it to interact with new concepts through socially and authentic experiences. These engaging and intentionally designed learning experiences empower students to own their learning by validating, confirming, contradicting, sharing, and extending the language of content.

"Tell me and I forget, teach me and I may remember, involve me and I learn." — *Benjamin Franklin*

SECTION II

Building Fluency in the Language of Content

$$E=MC^2$$

$$\pi = 3.14159265$$

$$V_f = V_i + at$$

$$a^2 + b^2 = c^2$$

$$H_2O$$

x

5 cm

90

$$M = 5.9736 \times 1024 \, kg$$

2, 3, 5, 7, 11, 13, 17, 19, 23, 29, 31, 37, 41, 43, 47, 53, 59, 61, 67, 71, 73, 79, 83, 89, 97

Chapter Three

Student Interest and Instructional Materials

Teachers can change lives with just the right mix of chalk and challenge. --Joyce Meyer

---

As we consider literacy in the context of today's world, it is important to note that what constitutes the definition of text is vastly changing. Society and technology continually change; literacy and texts change as well. Because technology has increased the complexity and connectedness of literate environments, a literate person must possess a wide range of abilities and competencies, with a wide range of materials. With the increased availability of information that can be accessed at the touch of a finger, it is important that students critically evaluate the sources and to do so they must be taught this process. Keep in mind as you read through this chapter that text refers to anything from which meaning can be acquired, that a message is carried in the content and not the form itself. For example, this includes books, signs, pictures, photos, media, and art.

Young children benefit from opportunities to read a rich array of both fiction and informational materials. Children like to learn about the world around them and welcome opportunities to see real images of things they can relate to and want to learn more about. Researchers agree that young children benefit from increased exposure to informational books and suggest that many children in kindergarten and first grade often prefer to read nonfiction books, but most often the genre of choice is fiction in the primary grades (Duke, 2014; Mohr, 2006; Pappas, 1993; Snow, Burns, & Griffin, 1998). Often there is very little nonfiction materials available in primary classrooms, and read-alouds are generally focused on fiction and readings with a narrative writing style (Duke & Bennett-Armistead, 2003).

So what about those children who have a preference for nonfiction? Many children are "info kids" and want to read informational texts and by the time students reach upper elementary grades, they are expected to read and learn from informational text and content area textbooks, yet they struggle due to lack of opportunity to learn reading strategies for nonfiction (Duke & Bennett-Armistead, 2003). Therefore, greater exposure to informational texts during the early years may help minimize difficulties in content area reading at the upper levels. Reading achievement increases as the diversity of reading experiences increases and children who reported reading a wide variety of text (e.g., narrative, informational) had higher reading achievement than students who reported reading only one type of text. Thus, it seems reasonable that exposing young children to informational text will help them to handle the literacy demands of their later schooling (Duke & Bennett-Armistead, 2003; Kristo & Bamford, 2004).

Another consideration for reading nonfiction is building of academic vocabulary. Most academic disciplines have their own language, which includes specialized words and phrases that have very specific meanings within the subject. For example, in language arts you will probably encounter words such as similes, metaphors, synonyms, adjectives, and so forth; whereas in biology, you will most likely learn about herbivores, carnivores, and omnivores. This being the case for each subject area makes it essential for students to have a strong foundation of academic vocabulary to understand concepts and also strategies to learn new vocabulary as they read and take in new information. Students with more developed academic vocabularies are more successful in content areas, because knowing the meanings of content-specific words helps readers more fully comprehend the material they will be reading (Duke, 2014). Later in the chapter we will read about some ways to support learning of academic vocabulary.

Matching Readers and Texts

How many times have you read something and just can't get interested in what you are reading? Did you understand or remember anything you read when you finished? Reader interest is vital to comprehension of virtually any written material (Hughes-Hassell & Lutz, 2006). In addition to interest, the attitude of the reader and prior knowledge are significant factors that contribute to reading comprehension. Therefore, these should be considered in the process of exploring texts and conditions under which a student will succeed in reading. Teachers must contemplate approaches to evaluating readers and matching student interests and needs with nonfiction texts. This requires teachers who can connect students with texts to be innovative and have confidence in exploring a vast array of materials, as well as instructional practices.

Assessment of students' interests and abilities to read and learn from nonfiction texts is an essential element in designing and planning effective instruction in content areas. For teachers to make appropriate instructional decisions they must have knowledge of how students will be expected to interact with and respond to nonfiction texts and other informational materials used as vehicles for instruction. Awareness of students' abilities and interest is paramount in selecting materials and planning for instruction as it would not be uncommon to find a range of reading ability among students that may well vary as much as five to eight grade levels in some classrooms. Such a range of reading levels can present challenges for teachers when selecting appropriate texts and materials for each individual reader.

Most young children learn to read using a combination of narrative style, fiction materials, and trade books. However, when reaching the middle grades a transition takes place from narrative storylines and trade book materials to expository style texts and content area textbook reading, yet students' abilities to transfer the reading skills learned and practiced in other genres cannot be assumed, and is often a factor attributed to a lack of reading achievement in content-specific areas. The problem with reading and comprehending nonfiction texts is often compounded by the selection of materials written on a readability level above the students' reading levels and with complex vocabulary and concepts that students must first build schema. In addition, nonfiction is written in an expository style, which is not only more difficult for many students to read, but for some it is less interesting than texts written in a narrative style.

There are two basic premises teachers can use to match readers to text. First, having a lot of knowledge about text is helpful, because "text matters" (Duke, 2014; Hiebert, 1999). Secondly, teachers must assess the reading level of students, as well as know the level of the text. These are necessary so that the right text or materials can be matched to the right reader at the correct time. With knowledge of texts and readers, teachers intuitively accomplish this match, which contributes to reader success. Matching readers with nonfiction texts can be trickier due to the academic vocabulary and the text features. You may refer back to chapter 2 to review the features of nonfiction that support learning of academic vocabulary and content. Some vocabulary presented in texts may be far too difficult for the readers. Also, some texts include so many features that it can be cumbersome for readers to know where to start reading on a page or the pages are visually overstimulating for some children.

When appropriate texts are selected that support many aspects of the reading process, the reader and text are truly matched. Readers benefit from teachers who take the time to understand more than just the reading level of the student, but also their interests, motivation, prior knowledge, developmental maturity, and purpose for reading. When students are matched to texts this creates an ideal context for reading practice and deepening comprehension where teachers can appropriately scaffold learning. The reality of this is twofold—from an objective perspective matching of text to reader increases comprehension of the text they read; and from a subjective perspective the reader's confidence, competence, and independence when reading increases. A match between reader and text makes reading pleasurable and productive versus a mismatch which makes readers discouraged and frustrated. The ultimate goal in matching readers with text is that readers choose to read, therefore reading more and with practice reading better.

For too long, many children have been provided materials that are not an appropriate level of difficulty for them. If students are to learn and apply reading strategies, they need texts that provide a good balance between support and challenge. That is, texts should be easy enough to develop confidence and self-assurance, while facilitating comprehension, yet difficult enough to provide some challenge to require the reader to do some "reading work" (Clay, 1991). The best teachers know their students and build upon individual strengths with just the right mix of success and challenge, soaring and wavering, clarity and ambiguity. You may think of this as a recipe for success. However, it can take many hours of professional practice to develop and refine this awareness of the lowest-level book to the highest, and to refine techniques for leveling readers. Teachers must know where students are and find material that will challenge them sufficiently without being so difficult that they lose motivation or become frustrated. This becomes more of a challenge in the upper primary grades as the choice of materials increases dramatically and the range in student reading levels widens.

Teachers can make effective "just right" reader-text matches with the right information. A "just right" text for independent reading is one in which a reader can read 95% to 100% of the words and fully comprehend the text. For instructional purposes, a "just right" text is one in which the reader can read about 90% to 95% of the words and comprehend the meaning with little degree of difficulty (Clay, 1991). More difficult text is considered to be at a reader's "frustration" level when they read fewer than 90% of the words as this inhibits comprehension and will require additional teacher support. The accompanying chart provides considerations for teachers when matching texts and readers.

KNOWING YOUR READERS	CONSIDERATIONS
Comprehension: What are the independent and instructional reading levels of my students? Is there a difference in fiction versus nonfiction reading for each student?	**Comprehension:** Running records, reading and conferencing with students, analyzing formal and informal data
Background knowledge: What does the student know about this topic to understand the content? What experiences have the students had with nonfiction text?	**Background knowledge:** Vocabulary on the topic, text structures, text features, visual images
Strategies: What strategies do the students use? Do they have a variety of strategies in their tool box?	**Strategies:** Before, during, and after reading strategies (see chart below for strategies to support reading)

CONSIDERATIONS ABOUT TEXTS
The text itself: How long is the text? What size is the font? What is the appearance and placement of print and images on the page? How complex is the concept? How many words are on a page?
Sentences: Are the sentences short or long? Are they simple or complex sentences?
Text structures: Does the text have organizational structures to support understanding of the content? Do the students know how to read various text structures? Have they been taught how to do so?
Features: Does the text have features that support understanding of the content? What features does the text have? Do students know how to use the features to develop understanding? Is there graphic support? If so, to what degree do charts and illustrations help the reader or become an obstacle to learning? Have the students been taught how to read graphics to support learning of the content?
Vocabulary: Is there new vocabulary that students need to know before reading? Is the vocabulary easy for the student to grasp, as well as the concept or is there a large amount of new vocabulary and difficult concepts which will require the students to need more support before and during reading? Are key words repeated throughout the text?

Keeping all of this in mind as we work with students to match readers and texts, our ultimate goal is to help students learn how to select texts that they can and want to read. So what are some ways we as teachers can do this? We must model the process over and over, as well as guide the students through the selection process. Let's see how this process might look.

- Students need to know that learning how to choose books is an important reading and life skill and that you will be teaching them more about book selection and the importance of choosing the "just right" text.
- Most importantly, students need time to select a text they think is right for them and that they are interested in reading. Too often students are

not provided adequate time to explore many texts before making text selections.

- Students should read aloud some of the text then ask themselves some questions. Is my reading fluent? Did I stop for punctuation and did I know most of the words? Did I understand what I was reading? Can I retell what I just read? Can I anticipate what might happen or what I might learn next?
- Students need to determine if the text was too hard, too easy, or just right and they need to be able to explain what made it so—the "why." A text may be too easy and not extend a student's learning with new information. On the other hand, the vocabulary may be too difficult and the text may not contain adequate text features to assist the student in understanding the academic vocabulary. Also, some texts contain so much information that it is difficult for students to know where to start reading—that is, there can be too many graphics and facts on a page. You may refer back to chapter 2 and review some of the text features that support learning of content and vocabulary.
- If needed, support the student in making another text selection. This process takes time to model and for students to learn to apply, but once they get it, they become independent in text selection.

Matching readers and texts is essential, but what do you do to support learning when they have the perfect text for them? Before, during, and after reading strategies support learning of academic vocabulary and content. Students need a variety of strategies throughout the reading process. Here are some strategies that you might consider. As you read through these imagine how this would look with your students when they have the perfect text to support learning. You may also refer back to some of these strategies as you read further about text sets and creating word walls.

Before Reading Strategies	
Predicting	Examine the cover illustration and read the title of new book. Ask students to predict what it might be about based on either the cover picture, the title, or both. Ask the reasoning behind their prediction and discuss their predictions.
Activating background knowledge/schema	Your schema is all the background knowledge and experiences that you have had. Ask the student to tell you what he or she knows about the subject, or to recall any experiences related to the subject.
Conduct a picture and text feature walk	Have the student look through the text and look at the pictures and take note of the text features that may help support understanding of content and academic vocabulary. Read the headings, captions, and vocabulary terms specific to the content.
Noticing structure of the text	Discuss the structure of the text and help students connect it with other similarly structured texts they have read.
Forming purpose for reading	Formulate and encourage the student to come up with two or three predictions or questions before reading.
During Reading Strategies	
Meaning or semantics	Readers use the features in nonfiction to figure out the vocabulary and content and to make sense of the text. Readers continually evaluate the information they take in to determine if it makes sense as they gain understanding.
Questioning	Too often questions are used only at the end of reading, to check comprehension, but successful readers ask themselves questions throughout the reading process.
Clarify and evaluate	As students read they should seek clarification and evaluate what they are learning. This includes confirming predictions, making new predictions, and connecting information while building schema.
After Reading Strategies	
Organize	Model ways that students can organize information as they take in new content and vocabulary to reinforce the concepts.
Summarize	Students should summarize their reading to determine understanding of key points and concepts using content vocabulary.
Levels of questioning	Encourage students to respond to different levels of questioning: • Factual or "right there" questions where answers are found directly in the text • Inference or "think and search" questions where students must look for evidence to support their thinking • "In my head" or "on my own" questions where students must use their knowledge and understanding to make connections and meaning

Text Sets in Your Classroom: Instructional Materials to Support Content Fluency

Now let's look at an instructional approach to support learning the language of content that can truly match texts and readers—text sets. So what are text sets and how do they support learning? Text sets are collections of resources and materials from a wide array of genre, media, and levels of reading difficulty, yet only focus on one concept or topic designed to be supportive of readers with a range of skills, experiences, and interests. They can be centered on an anchor text with other texts included for instructional support to create meaningful connections and deepen understanding. By assembling materials ranging from fiction to nonfiction and poetry, from videos to maps and charts, articles to historical documents, websites, photographs, songs, and paintings, teachers can add depth, voice, and perspectives to the study of any concept, topic, or complex issue. You may think of a well-selected set of materials as texts "talking to one another" so as students read the texts they build knowledge about a specific topic.

Text sets are especially important for students where the whole class is using a single textbook or the same text. Additionally, a well-planned and well-developed text set provides all students—regardless of reading level or learning style—a "way in" to access information about specific concepts or content. When learning about new or complex topics even competent adult learners seek "easy books" or materials to build knowledge or understanding of a subject. We Google or search for explanations, definitions, or information that is written in more simple terms or look for pictures to build schema on difficult subjects. Therefore, we must provide children with the same opportunities to see and read a variety of materials in terms they can connect to and understand. When teachers make the transition from relying on textbooks to including multi-texts, the focus of study becomes concepts or topics where students gain both a broad perspective and in-depth experience of the subject matter by reading many texts on the same topic. Think about the textbooks you have read in science or social studies. They cover a wide array of concepts with basic information on each topic. No single textbook contains an adequate amount of information to help student's become even mildly expert on any topic.

EXAMPLES OF ACCESSIBLE TEXTS

- Novels
- Picture books
- Poems
- Nonfiction
- Fiction
- Newspaper articles
- Short stories
- Vignettes
- Biographical information
- Internet pieces
- Websites
- Student writing
- Mathematical writing
- Lists
- Historical recounts
- Photographs
- Cartoons
- Quotes
- Song lyrics
- Stamps
- Letters and journals
- Pictures of artwork
- Calendars
- Recipes
- Brochures
- Almanacs
- Maps
- Charts and graphs
- Catalogs
- Menus

The use of text sets provides a way to have books rub up against other books and spark wonderful conversations. By having multiple books on a topic students have the opportunity to hear different people—that is, the people behind the books—which is important. Text sets can help students explore new questions or revisit ideas and concepts. However they are used, students need time to choose and read the texts, then share what they have read in some way. Students should make connections between texts and find patterns, moving from predictions, initial stereotypes, and presumptions to broader pools of talk and meaning making.

Let's highlight some of the benefits of text sets before we look at selecting materials and assembling them.

Text sets can provide multiple perspectives on a wide array of concepts and complex issues.
Learners at all ability levels and learning styles can be successful with text sets that have a good variety of selections and reading levels.
They are a good way to enrich the curriculum and content without the great expense of purchasing costly materials.
Students begin the inquiry process as they develop questions about a topic and use a variety of resources to find answers to their questions.
Including multi-texts in a set affords students opportunities for intertextual reading, to make text to text connections, and reflect on other texts they have experienced, such as movies or television shows, and through the process they are building and constructing new knowledge through shared discourse.
Higher level thinking is supported through text sets as students develop the ability to read multiple forms of texts. Refer to the list noted on the sidebar of the many possibilities of texts that may be included to provide a vast array of reading experiences.
By including an array of selections to support a concept or topic students have choice in what they read, the order in which they read to construct knowledge, and how they plan to use and share the information.
The intent of text sets is not to "catch" kids who aren't reading, they are designed to give all readers a choice of interesting and accessible text. They provide opportunities for learning and practicing reading strategies.

When teachers create text sets they should go through a purposeful planning process, thinking about a theme from many perspectives. Teachers should ask themselves questions, such as:

- What are the interests of my students?
- What do my students know about this topic?
- What do I want my students to know about this topic?
- Why is this concept or topic important?
- Am I including materials from various perspectives and genres?
- Are varying voices heard through the texts?
- Do I have a variety of texts to support learning?
- How will this text set help my students build knowledge about the topic?

Assembling and Arranging Text Sets: Some Things to Think About

Now that you have an understanding of the benefits of text sets and questions to ponder, let's look at the process of assembling and arranging text sets. So what's the best way to arrange text sets? How do you assemble a text set? What are some things to consider when creating a collection? What drives the text set?

Selecting texts for teaching can be a complex process. There is no single process for creating text sets; teachers may take a variety of approaches given their purpose, goals, and available resources. For instance, a teacher may first identify an anchor text and then plan an overall topic of inquiry for the set or they may choose to first identify a concept or topic for a unit of study and then seek an anchor text around which to build the set, then add other supplemental materials. In choosing your texts, you will want to consider the features of strong text sets to determine whether a text is worthy of inclusion in the set. Making sure the text contributes to the balance of text genres and is worthy of student time and attention. It is important that teachers continually refine, research, and reflect on text sets to determine the benefit for students. It is an ongoing process, not a once and done.

Although all students benefit from text sets, in some cases, you may want to create a set to support developing readers by building knowledge and vocabulary around a topic prior to in-depth inquiry. Therefore, you may consider creating a small set with a few texts that are at lower reading levels, yet another strategy for supporting developing readers is to use a gradated text set. This refers to a set in which text difficulty demands a steady increase to build understanding and reading strategies closer to grade level. However in other instances, you may want to provide an opportunity for students to build on the knowledge they have gained from exploring a topic and consider a set that includes several titles at more challenging levels of complexity.

Think about your students and what would interest or engage them. The collection should include a range of texts differentiated by their genres and format all on the same topic that any student would be able to follow an interest and access the material. The text sets you assemble should demonstrate the possibilities to the students, therefore you must strike a balance in materials. A slim collection may not inspire students to explore, whereas a really large collection might intimidate students. Additionally, if you have a number of English language learners or special education students, it is important to try to locate a picture dictionary, copy and include the pages particular to your concept in the set as a reference.

Text sets should be arranged so they are accessible to all students. They can be placed in reading centers or other areas where students can peruse them and take a text to read independently or through shared reading. Plastic tubs or baskets are a great means for organizing and displaying the materials. Students can easily take the entire tub and sit on the floor to explore and read through several texts to compare and analyze the content.

Considerations in Creating a Text Set

1. Reading must be purposeful and meaningful, therefore you must make purposeful decisions in selecting materials. Take advantage of all resources available from the library to technology. Be sure you are selecting high-quality resources and not just the first texts you locate. Evaluate them based on content, readability, and engagement for students.
2. The resources in your text set MUST address many reading levels. Even your most advanced reader will enjoy reading picture books as well as those with more of a challenge. The text set is for everyone's use so you will need an extremely wide range of material.
3. Your text set MUST have a wide variety of resources. Remember to include resources that will appeal to ALL of your students' interests. Match students to the texts you include.
4. You must know children's literature and read what they read. Don't forget to look through the children's and young adult magazines. These magazines are usually themed and could provide you with an inspiration for a text set! Additionally, a text set topic or concept can become the cornerstone for another text set.
5. You must LOVE what you are creating! Think about options because this is going to take a lot of time, effort, and planning on your part. You want your passion for the concept or topic of the text set to be very apparent to your students. Your enthusiasm and interest will spill over to them.
6. This is your opportunity to teach students about a CONCEPT. So if you want students to understand the concept of life in the desert, you would

include plants, animals, artwork, maps, stories, etc., anything that would help students think in many directions about life in a desert.

7. Read the newspaper every day and watch the news. You will find many possibilities lurking in local events and places in students' own backyard. Current events are a great resource!

8. An important consideration is that text sets should grow and change with your curriculum. New texts should be added and current ones replaced. As your topic of study changes so should your text set (Ivey, 2002).

Let's look at some texts you may include in a set, why each piece is a good selection, and how you might use them.

Here are some examples of tools to include to get a text set started about the solar system. These texts are appropriate for second to third grade:

Auguilar, D. A. (2011), *13 Planets: The Latest View of the Solar System* (National Geographic Kids). Washington DC: National Geographic Children's Books, 64 pages.

What is this—13 planets? This book provides a broader look at the solar system than the typical focus on the eight largest planets. Pluto was no longer a planet, then some categorized it as a dwarf planet along with Ceres and Eris, and then comes Haumea and Makemake, too! The recent discussions of the International Astronomical Union have outdated every solar system book. To address this the National Geographic joined forces with David Aguilar of the Harvard Smithsonian Astronomical Observatory to revise their 2008 book to provide young readers with a more current look at the solar system and space. The text is simple and includes photorealistic computer art. This nonfiction book describes the 13 planets, in their newly created categories, along with the Sun, clouds, comets, and other worlds that are being discovered every day in other galaxies. The book presents how the solar system was formed and then progresses to a discussion of each individual planet, the Sun, and comets all while using appropriate scientific terminology (definitions of bolded words can be found in the glossary). This book is useful for researching exact information and classifications of the planets in the solar system. Children will be able to not only find information from side notes on each page but will also be able to flip back to the glossary and reference pages to find out information such as the diameter of each planet, number of rings each planet has, number of moons, etc. (Amazon.com)

Cole, J. (1992). *The Magic School Bus Lost in the Solar System*. New York: Scholastic, 40 pages.

This text can be considered a hybrid text as it intertwines both fiction and nonfiction in a children's book that narrates a field trip with Ms. Frizzle's class to the planetarium only to find that it is closed. As they return to school their bus begins to act oddly, sending them rocketing towards a journey in outer space. Although the story is fictional, it is full of accurate information about gravity, the Sun, and the planets orbiting around the Sun, making this story very beneficial in a unit study over the solar system. This book is useful in providing factual information in the midst of a fictional story where students can build vocabulary and background knowledge of the solar system. (Amazon.com)

Ornes, S., "Distant 'Goldilocks' World," Science News for Kids. 21 Dec. 2011. sciencenewsforkids.org/2011/distant-'goldilocks'-world/

This article discusses the finding of a newly discovered planet that looks as if it could possibly support life. It presents information as to the average temperature of the planet as well as its size and orbital pattern. The article includes ideas and debates on the possible terrain that the new planet may hold and if there is even a remote possibility that it would be able to sustain life. At the end of the article the author includes "power words" for readers to reference if they are unable to determine the meaning of one of the power words in context. This would be a great piece to use in discussion of how technology continues to help us grow and learn as a society. There are also links to other articles that support the content. (Amazon.com)

Rabe, T. (1999), *There's No Place Like Space: All About Our Solar System* (Cat in the Hat's Learning Library). New York: Random House Books for Young Readers, 48 pages.

This is a fictional children's book, which includes basic vocabulary and terminology that is found in all space texts. The book has colorful and whimsical illustrations that will engage students. The book also has a glossary for the students to reference and an index showing where a subject can be found in the book. This book is useful in comparing actual photographs of space and space shuttles to that depicted in a Dr. Seuss manner. The book contains a glossary full of terms that could be included in word walls during the unit of study. (Amazon.com)

Seymour, S. (2007). *Our Solar System* (revised edition). New York: Harper Collins, 72 pages.

This nonfiction children's book takes readers on a journey through the nine planets, moons, asteroids, meteoroids, and comets that orbit around the Sun. (There are only eight planets now as Pluto was declassified as a planet, thus this would be a great text to prompt discussion of why it is no longer considered a planet and how previous texts can become inaccurate with the discovery of new information or changes in what defines a planet.) Many authentic photographs of the solar system and the objects that are found in it are included, which is appropriate for students age 6 and up. The book takes the reader through every feature found in our solar system and explains in terms easy for students to understand from the history to the future. This book is useful for developing understanding about the solar system on a deeper level than just planets and moons. The text includes topics such as black holes and the Milky Way. Features of the book to support content are charts and diagrams showing where everything would be in its orbit around the Sun. (Amazon.com)

Vogt, G. (2012). *Scholastic Reader 2: Solar System.* Scholastic Paperbacks.

In this nonfiction text the author provides basic information needed about the solar system for readers. This book goes into depth about each planet as well as the Sun. The reader is given an abundance of information about each planet, such as its location and size. Definitions of important vocabulary words that pertain to the solar system, such as gravity, are included. Students can make connections as they read this larger print text and build knowledge as they explore. (Amazon.com)

Our Solar System: A Poem to Teach Children, by Kurt Chambers

The moon shines so very bright, especially on a crisp clear night.
The Sun is big and very hot, and also covered in little spots.

Mercury is indeed quite small, against the Sun it's a tiny ball.
Venus is cloudy like a rainy day, but much too hot to go out and play.

The Earth is blue and warm and nice, and this is where I spend my life.
Mars is next and oh so red, there's no life, and it's completely dead.

Jupiter is the biggest of them all, but it's just a giant gas ball.
Saturn looks cool with its enormous ring, it's the solar systems ultimate bling-bling.

Uranus always gets a laugh, but it really isn't quite that daft.
Neptune is next upon the list, with its almost invisible disc.

Now we've come so very far, from our friendly yellow star, we come to Pluto which some do say, is not a planet anyway.

Planet Lineup from the Sun	Published on May 13, 2014
Our Planets revolve around the sun, Here they go one by one. There once were nine planets you know, But poor little Pluto had to go. Now with eight we're looking great, Let's learn the order, we must not wait! First in line from the sun, Mercury comes in at one. Mercury is very small, And looks like a rough, rocky ball. Venus is number two in line, Nice and bright and doing fine. The air is hot as it rotates slow, Clouds above hide what's below. Our own Earth is number three, We call it home, you and me! As it spins round and round, Gravity keeps our feet on the ground. Fourth in line is our red Mars, Rotating amongst the stars. Named for a Roman god of war, Many think it's ready to explore. Number five is Jupiter, With clouds around it in a stir. It's the largest one of all, Shining like a giant ball. Saturn is our number six, Around it clouds and dust do mix. Rings around the planet turn, An interesting planet that Saturn. Uranus is seven in line, Spinning around in its own time. Blue and green it appears they say, Maybe we'll get a closer look one day. We don't know much about Neptune, But that is has a large frozen moon. Coming in at number eight, One big dark spot notes its fate! As was stated once before, Pluto joins them no more! History has really changed you see, For years before there were nine they believe.	 https://www.youtube.com/watch?v=F2prtmPEjOc F2prtmPEjOideo I am the Sun. I'm a burning ball of fire. I'm very big indeed. Life on earth depends on me. I am the Sun. I am Mercury. I'm the closest planet to the Sun. I'm a ball of iron -- I have no moons. I am Mercury. I am Venus. I'm the same size as the Earth but I spin the other way and much more slowly. I have no water -- I am Venus. I am the Earth. The place where we all live. There is land and lots of sea so I look blue. I have a moon. I am the Earth. I am Mars. I'm a rocky, red planet. My mountains are the highest in our solar system. I have two moons. I am Mars. I am Jupiter. I'm a gas giant. I'm the biggest and I spin the fastest. I have the biggest moon. I am Jupiter. I am Saturn. I'm a gas giant. My rings are made of ice. Titan is my biggest moon. I am Saturn. I am Uranus. I'm an icy gas giant. I'm the coldest planet in our solar system. And I have rings made of dust. I am Uranus. I am Neptune. I'm an icy gas giant. I'm the farthest planet from the sun. I have many storms. I am Neptune. We are The Solar System.

Looking at the list noted in the sidebar, what other texts or materials might you include to develop this set further? What other resources or genres will you seek to make this well rounded?

Another Approach to Text Sets: Literature Circles

Literature circles are small literature discussion groups where students gather to share thoughts and ideas about a piece of literature. It is an in-depth process and is guided by students' response to what they have read. Literature circles provide a way for students to engage in critical thinking and reflect as they read, discuss, and respond to texts. Students reshape, add to their knowledge, change ways of thinking, and develop deeper understanding as they construct meaning with other readers. The discussion is led by the students; they decide how much to read and the roles each member will be responsible for each session. Students become engaged as a community of learners negotiating meaning of the readings by their experiences and the shared experiences of their group members. So let's think about this process with a text set. We have discussed the fact that text sets are centered on a specific concept of topic and the reading levels vary. Now let's look at the process with clustered texts on a topic.

Consider developing a text set around the topic of World War II for fifth- or sixth-grade students. In the process you will select many different texts for students to explore, but students may also participate in literature circles related to the central theme. Once you have determined your topic, then seek a variety of texts to support the content and the readers. For example, look at the texts below and the descriptions of each. All are related to the topic of WWII; however, some are longer in length and are written at more advanced reading levels. Some have more pictures, graphs, maps, and charts for support. Students can be grouped based on reader/text match, yet all are learning some common academic vocabulary and developing understanding of the overall concept of the unit of study. Consider the terms *atomic bomb, leukemia, concentration camp, Nazi, Jew, Hitler, capture,* and *evacuation* that are common in each of the texts. (Vocabulary that is specific to the content can be supported through word walls, which you will read about a little later in this chapter.) Students also learn geography from Japan, to Pearl Harbor, from France to Sweden, and Germany to the United States. Students are learning content through all subject areas through a combination of text sets and literature circles. Although literature circles are centered on small-group discussions in this instance, students can come together and have a grand conversation about what they are reading, making text to text connections from the readings of each group and students are using common vocabulary specific to the content.

Sadako and the Thousand Paper Cranes, by Eleanor Coerr and Ronald Himler, recommended for grades 3–7, ages 8–12, 80 pages. This story is based on the true story of a young Japanese girl, Sadako, who is diagnosed with leukemia as a result of the atom bomb that was dropped on Hiroshima. The story follows Sadako from a healthy schoolgirl winning races, through her diagnosis with the atom bomb sickness, and finally her long stay in the hospital. It is in the hospital that she first begins making origami cranes to pass the time. Her goal is to make 1,000 cranes.

Number the Stars, by Lois Lowry, recommended for grades 4–7, ages 9–12, 156 pages. One of the great untold stories of World War II is the evacuation of Jews from Nazi-controlled Denmark. On September 29, 1943, word spread in Denmark that Jews were to be detained and sent to the death camps. Through the eyes of 10-year-old Annemarie, readers learn of the Danish Resistance, which results in smuggling almost the entire Jewish population of Denmark, nearly 7,000 people, across the sea to Sweden.

The Journey that Saved Curious George: The True Wartime Escape of Margret and H. A. Rey, by Louise Borden and Allan Drummond, recommended for grades 4–7, ages 9–12, 80 pages. In 1940, Hans and Margret Rey fled their Paris home fearing the advancement of the German army. They began their dreadful journey on bicycles, pedaling to Southern France with children's book manuscripts and pictures among their few possessions in tow. Cycling day to day and boarding train after train as the Nazis occupied Paris, they finally sailed to Rio and then on to New York, where Curious George was published within a year.

Who Was Anne Frank?, by Ann Abramson and Nancy Harrison, recommended for grades 4–7, ages 9–12, 112 pages. *The Diary of Anne Frank* revealed the treacherous life that her family endured in hiding during World War II. This text focuses closely on Anne's life before the secret annex, including what life was like in hiding, and the legacy of her diary. The text includes black-and-white illustrations, maps, and diagrams to provide historical and visual reference.

Faithful Elephants: A True Story of Animals, People and War, recommended for grades 4–6, ages 8–12, 32 pages. A zookeeper narrates the story of John, Tonky, and Wanly, three performing elephants at the Ueno Zoo in Tokyo. When bombs showered Tokyo in the bleak days of World War II, zookeepers were ordered to destroy the animals for the safety of others. The zookeepers weep and pray that the war would end so their beloved elephants might be saved.

Evaluating Text Sets

As you begin to think of ways to create a text set and explore resources, it is also important to evaluate your final product. What makes a text set strong and what makes it weaker? Although there can be some benefit to students from a weaker set, the connections between some of the texts are often superficial or vague, and it is not clear how a teacher might use the texts to support the building of knowledge for students. A stronger set is more focused and related texts are connected concretely by the topic or concept. Strong sets provide a rich context for close, analytic reading, comparison, and synthesis of texts through which students are more likely to gain knowledge, vocabulary, and develop a process of inquiry about a selected topic.

To determine the strength of your text set in supporting content language and knowledge acquisition it is important to evaluate student use and responses to the materials. This can be accomplished in a variety of ways First of all, just observing students as they interact with the sets will help you assess whether or not they are using all of the materials or if they prefer some texts over others to explore and gain knowledge. Another way to evaluate is to have students compare and contrast pieces in the text set and recording in a journal or create a graphic organizer to demonstrate understanding.

When exploring a text set it can be helpful to have questions recorded for students to ponder and research as they read and in doing so the use of sticky notes can help students note interesting and important places in the text. Students may use journals to write their own connections they made or new understandings they have after reading the materials. Just listening in on group discussions before, during, and after reading and sharing materials can be the most helpful in determining the effectiveness of each of the selected materials individually, as well as the text set as a whole in building content knowledge and academic vocabulary. Through observations and text use you will know if students are engaged in the set and want to read the materials to gain knowledge. So let's look at a comparison of strong and weak text sets to help you become more evaluative when creating them for your students.

Features of Strong Text Sets	Features of Weak Text Sets
Text builds student knowledge about a topic and academic vocabulary.	Text does not support learning of topic for students.
Text is meaningfully related or connected to other texts in the set.	Text is not related or connected, or is only superficially linked to other texts.
Text is rich, authentic, worthy of reading, and engaging.	Text is poorly selected and lacks depth and engagement for students.
Text includes a range of genres and formats.	Text is focused on one genre almost exclusively.
Complexity of text supports student reading levels and provides a staircase effect to support gradual increase in reading more complex texts to support content acquisition and reading strategies.	Complexity is erratic and does not support a staircase effect of complexity to build content knowledge and reading strategies.

BECOMING FLUENT IN THE LANGUAGE OF CONTENT

Word Walls: Supporting Vocabulary Acquisition and Content Fluency

An interactive and engaging classroom environment greatly influences learning and in particular literacy development (Wolfersberger, Reutzel, Sudweeks, & Fawson, 2004). When you are in a doctor's office or other waiting rooms, do you read all of the things that are displayed on the walls (e.g., signs, posters, pictures, inspirational quotes)? Most often our eyes are drawn to the various texts and images around the room. The same holds true for children in a classroom. Their eyes are drawn to colorful displays of pictures and words. You can walk by most any classroom and see children staring at things on the walls, making connections and learning. These displays are invitations to think, by allowing students to focus on new, exciting, and engaging learning opportunities. Now let's look at another way to support learning of new topics or concepts that connects well with the content of texts sets.

Among the features that have become common displays in classrooms are word walls, because they have proven to be effective tools in building children's knowledge of words. Although a variety of strategies should be implemented to introduce children to new vocabulary and build understanding of concepts, studies show that there are many benefits for children when teachers use word walls (Christ & Wang, 2010; Harmon, Wood, Hedrick, Vintinner, & Willeford, 2009; Jasmine & Schiesl, 2009; Neuman & Dwyer, 2009; Wasik, 2006).

You may wonder how displaying a bunch of words on the wall of a classroom helps children build knowledge of words. It's not that simple; there is so much more to the process. What better way to support leaning of academic vocabulary than displaying words in your classroom for students to easily access? Imagine what a word wall on the topics noted above in the text set section might look like. Can you picture a word wall on the vocabulary specific to WWII or the solar system? Having word walls available is not enough, however; children should be actively engaged in using them to support acquisition of new vocabulary. Word walls are for children to refer to when learning about a new topic, which is an important tool in teaching vocabulary and reading to children. Brabham and Villaume (2001) present three purposes of word walls: to facilitate word analyses, to model the correct spelling of words, and to help build vocabulary from various units of study. Word walls are a source of support and a point of reference for language and literacy learning that empower both students and teachers. They can enhance the literacy environment (Neuman & Dwyer 2009) where teachers are able to complement core curriculum with supplemental vocabulary instruction.

Word walls have the potential to help students develop ownership and individual control of reading, transitioning from teacher support to independent reading. When children are participants in creating and maintaining word walls, they play a vital role in their own learning (Jackson & Henrichs, 2012). According to Beck, McKeown, and Kucan (2013), when teachers include well-planned word wall activities children's comprehension and fluency in the words displayed is improved. Effective word wall activities provide opportunities to build word recognition by combining visual and active engagement with the words. Also important, teachers must select and implement developmentally appropriate word walls and activities to support literacy development in all content areas. There are endless possibilities when it comes to word walls. Teachers use them in different ways according to their own interpretations and the needs of the students. Consideration must be given to what type of word wall is best suited for the concept and purpose (Harmon et al., 2009).

How do word walls support learning and literacy?

Let's look at some ways that these tools effectively support literacy and learning in a variety of ways.

- Written words provide a visual image that can trigger short-term memory to help children with spelling.
- Students can learn high-frequency words, which develops sight vocabulary—those irregularly spelled words that don't follow the rules of phonics. By mastering frequently used words students don't have to decode each word as they read; and these sight words are stored in their long-term memory, which also builds reading fluency.
- Beginning readers benefit from word walls that show general principles of how words work and the relationship between words—that is, word families.
- Students can learn the rules of language, types of words, language conventions, and exceptions to rules.
- Displaying words allows students to become more independent as readers and writers, experimenting and problem solving.
- Students can learn new vocabulary and make connections to concepts. Vocabulary specific to content area learning is essential in understanding new topics. Word walls help students build schema as they make connections.

Varieties of word walls

There are many different kinds of word walls and it is important that teachers consider the best approach to support learning. Teachers must determine which word walls are most beneficial for the students in their class. Consideration must be given to the topic of study, interest and suggestions of students, skill level of students, most appropriate way to display the words, the purpose, and the instructional support the word wall will provide. Presented in the table are some options that teachers may consider.

Type of Word Wall	What It Looks Like	Instructional Support
ABC-letter and/or picture	A word for each letter of the alphabet posted on the wall and often an image of the word is displayed as well. A very basic way to introduce new vocabulary for a new concept or topic of study. This can be expanded to a picture dictionary by including multiple pictures with each letter.	This is an especially effective means for second language learners and emergent readers to learn new vocabulary and make connections between speaking, reading, and writing.
Around the door	Words are displayed around the door frame, door facings, or the actual door. This is a space in the classroom that can often be unused yet provides an engaging opportunity for students to see words displayed in a unique manner.	Words displayed can build on a topic or be presented in a sequential order, such as the water cycle. Students can reinforce understanding of words and concepts while in line or during transitioning times.
Ceiling or hanging	Words are displayed directly on the ceiling of hanging from the ceiling.	Specific concepts can be displayed that help support content area learning. Words and images for clouds, weather, or the solar system can be displayed around the room to build a broader and more realistic feel.
Traveling word walls	These are not really word walls, but are portable lists of words that can travel with students to and from their desks, between centers, or anywhere else the student may need the support. They can include words and pictures.	These can be used to provide individualized support by having specific words the student needs assistance with on a personal list. Traveling words walls may be created with specific words related to content area topics that students can take to their desk to learn, develop understanding, or use in writing.
Word stairs	Words are displayed in the form of stairs, the last letter of each word becomes the first letter of the next word and the words alternate from horizontal to vertical with the addition of each new word.	This type of word wall can be used to support critical thinking. Students can be challenged to find a word that connects with the content, but also has to begin with the letter that ends another word on the topic.

Graphic organizer	Words are displayed in various types of graphic organizers, a central theme is presented, and topics or concepts that are connected to the central theme are displayed around it.	Students can see words and think about a number of concepts that connect around a larger concept. (Refer to the texts noted above for literature circles—the center of a graphic organizer might have WWII with extending branches and bubbles of all of the vocabulary that students are learning through their readings and discussions.)
Personal	The alphabet is written in a folder for students to add words that they need to know that begin with each letter.	Students can find words quickly and add to their personal list of words that support their learning. This folder can be continually updated. The list of words can be general or content specific for units of study.

Some word walls can be helpful for all students and others may be too difficult. For example, with younger children an ABC word wall may be very appropriate, but a word stairs wall would be far too difficult. For a group of students with a wide range of reading levels, traveling word walls may be the best approach to address individual needs. Some children may benefit from engaging displays in unique areas such as the ceiling or around the door. Look closely at all areas of your classroom to determine the best place for a collections of words and the most appropriate type of word wall. What areas do students see daily that may engage them? What type of display would work best for the area selected? Where are areas in your classroom that need attention to make the environment more engaging? Most importantly, let the students create and develop the area. If they are part of it then they will own it and use the word walls.

Something to Think About!

Teachers wear a lot of hats and make important decisions every day about teaching and learning. It can be a challenge to meet the needs of every student, but if you take the time to really get to know your students, their interests, their strengths and needs, the support that they need to move to the next level, and their motivation to learn, then you are better equipped to make the right decision. A great teacher is constantly assessing and, therefore, making it easier to match readers and texts and seeking instructional approaches that help students become more independent in their learning. Word walls and text sets are two instructional approaches that can be adapted to all students and any grade level. Now that you have read about these approaches, and hopefully have thought of some ways you can use them in your classroom, remember there is not one recipe—these approaches are not specific to a subject area and they never look the same from year to year, month to month, or even from day to day. The reason? Real engagement with great literature encircled by a community of learners cannot be prescribed, it can only be described.

This is at the heart of all good education, where the teacher asks the students to think and engages them in encouraging dialogues, constantly checking for growth and understanding. —William Glasser

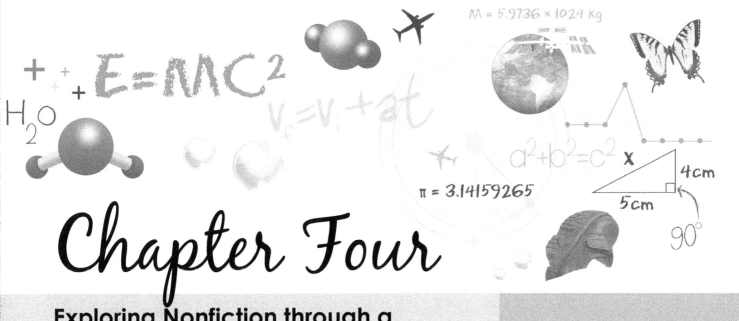

Chapter Four

Exploring Nonfiction through a Critical Lens

*Nonfiction writers are the packhorses of literature.
We're meant to carry the story. If we can make it up
and down the mountain by a reliable if not scenic route,
we have delivered. — Stacy Schiff*

Why Nonfiction?

Schools have always taught social studies and science, as well as literature, but emphasis has generally been on fiction-focused literacy with a little sprinkling of reading and writing in other subject areas. Children's reading and writing has most often been composed of make-believe, fictional stories; however, increased pressure of high stakes testing and the importance of informational reading in the upper grades has led to a greater emphasis on nonfiction in the early grades. Additionally, students today are often digitally connected and most online reading is nonfiction. We may think of this as the nonfiction revolution (Duke, 2014).

It is common knowledge that how often and how much a child reads is important, but with so many distractions competing for children's time and attention it can be a challenge to get children to simply open a book — any book (Duke, 2014). Children who read more have greater vocabulary and develop more complex thinking, so we want them to read a lot, but what children read is equally important. In order to develop a solid foundation for future learning, educators agree that students should begin reading informational texts in all subjects from the time they enter school versus waiting until the upper grades to place emphasis on expository reading. Non-fiction reading helps children develop more complex thinking and builds background for a variety of topics.

Nonfiction is everywhere in the world around us. The challenge is to find nonfiction texts that interest children, ones that are engaging and appropriate for the child's reading level. The goal is to get them to read nonfiction daily and actually enjoy it! While reading fiction is a great way to develop children's creativity and imagination, it is nonfiction that ignites their curiosity and opens their minds to the world around them.

Because children most often are exposed to a greater amount of fiction, it is important for students to understand the difference between fiction and nonfiction before diving in and learning about text structures and features. The format and flow of fiction is much easier to follow than nonfiction; however, once students understand how to navigate nonfiction they find much support in learning the content and finding answers to their questions. Fiction texts include characters, problems, and solutions—all of which are not included in nonfiction texts. Also, the pictures in fiction are not realistic compared to real photographs or more realistic drawings that are often featured in nonfiction. As noted on the verso page or copyright page, the Library of Congress catalogues fiction texts as "fiction," yet nonfiction is catalogued as "Juvenile Literature." This is very helpful in determining the type of text you are reading or selecting for your students, as well as for students to understand where to look for information about a text. Students need to understand the difference between fiction and nonfiction before they can understand the structures of various nonfiction texts. Let's look at the structures of the two genres.

Structures or Organization	
Fiction	**Nonfiction**
Story Elements: • Characters • Setting • Plot • Problem • Solution • Theme	Six Structures: • Cause and effect • Question/answer • Sequence or chronological • Description • Compare and contrast • Problem/solution

Fiction texts typically have literary elements as noted in the chart and as children hear and read stories they internalize the elements of fiction. They expect that there will be characters, interaction between characters, and some will be more important than others. Readers also expect a resolution to the problem that provides a satisfying ending. However, understanding the language of content is completely different. There is no flow to the information or story line, yet there are structures, signal words, and phrases that help the reader readily identify the author's intention, which will better equip them to understand the text as a whole.

What Are Text Structures?

Nonfiction text structures refer to HOW an author organizes information in a nonfiction or expository text. When introduced to a new text, students can determine the organizational pattern of the text by looking for cues to differentiate and identify which text structure was used by the author (Dymock, 2005). By pinpointing the structure of a text, students can then organize their thinking as a reader to match the structure of the text, which allows for more effective comprehension of the subject matter at hand. When students learn to distinguish the underlying structure of nonfiction texts, it helps them focus their attention on key concepts, vocabulary, connecting to background knowledge, and monitor their comprehension as they read.

As readers construct meaning through interaction with a text, their comprehension is facilitated when they organize their thinking in a method similar to the author. Readers who struggle with text comprehension of nonfiction often fail to recognize the organizational structure of what they are reading and they are not aware of signals that can alert them to particular text structures (Dymock & Nicholson, 2010).

All texts are different to a certain extent; however, depending upon the author's purpose, the topic, and the genre, nonfiction reading selections tend to be organized in specific structural patterns. These patterns should be explicitly taught to help students comprehend texts more effectively and to do so they must learn to analyze the structure of various texts structures (Dymock & Nicholson, 2010). Understanding nonfiction text structures is critical for "reading to learn"—that is, reading to gain understanding of information. Students should be aware of the six most common text structures and be able to identify each structure using signal words and key features. Understanding which text structure the author used helps students monitor their understanding of the reading, while learning the specific content and vocabulary (Dymock, 2005).

Before we look at the structural analysis of nonfiction texts, let's take a look at the many different types of nonfiction that readers may encounter. This may help as you learn about the various structures and be better equipped to determine what structure an author may use for each of these types of texts to convey meaning. As you can see from the following list, there is a plethora of nonfiction texts and there is much more than is noted here.

Types of Nonfiction

Albums	Documents	Newspaper
Almanac	Encyclopedia	Photograph
Autobiography	Essay	Photographic essay
Biography	Experiments	Reference
Blueprint	Handbooks	Research reports
Book report	How to books	Scientific paper
Creative nonfiction	Journal	Speech
Design document	Letter	Survey
Diagram	Literary criticism	Technical manuals
Diary	Magazine	Textbook
Dictionary	Map	Travelogue
Documentary film	Memoir	User manual
		Website

Text Structures and Signal Words

Now that you have an idea of the differences in fiction and nonfiction, as well as the wide variety of nonfiction materials, let's look closely at the six types of text structures. In doing so, see if you can think of texts that would meet the criteria for each structure. What structure would be a best fit for various authors' purposes? What topics or subject matter would best be presented through each of the structures?

A strategy that authors use to help readers understand the main points of their text is the use of "signal words." Signal words in a text suggest its structure and when students are aware of these words, it helps them identify and follow the text structure as the writer of the text intended. Signal words are important for readers as they link ideas together, show relationships, and help transition from one idea to the next. Each text structure is associated with different signal words, so let's consider the most common kinds of text structure based on purpose and some of the signal words used for each. You may also make connections to the types and purposes of word walls noted in chapter three; including signal words for each of the text structures in a word wall would be a wonderful tool for students when determining text structure.

Text Structure	Purpose	Signal Words	
Description	Provides information describing a topic, idea, person, place, or thing by listing its features, characteristics, or examples.	☐ Look for the topic word to be repeated ☐ For instance ☐ Such as… ☐ To begin with	☐ To illustrate ☐ Characteristics ☐ For example ☐ Looks like ☐ Appears to be ☐ An example
Compare and Contrast	Presents similarities and differences between two or more topics or concepts.	☐ Same as ☐ Similar to ☐ Likewise ☐ Alike ☐ Compared with ☐ As well as ☐ Not only…but also	☐ Both ☐ In common ☐ Instead of ☐ Either…or ☐ On the other hand ☐ Different from ☐ As opposed to
Sequence or Chronological	Events are described in numerical or chronological order or presents the steps to follow to do something or make something.	☐ First ☐ Second ☐ Third ☐ Next ☐ Then ☐ Before ☐ Initially ☐ After ☐ Afterword	☐ Finally ☐ Following ☐ Not long after ☐ Now ☐ Soon ☐ Today ☐ Until ☐ On…(date)
Problem/Solution	Problem is presented and often states why there is a problem, followed by one or more possible solutions.	☐ A problem ☐ A solution ☐ May be due to ☐ Steps involved ☐ If…then ☐ One reason is	☐ Question is ☐ Dilemma is ☐ For this reason ☐ To solve this ☐ One answer is
Cause/Effect	Cause is why something happened and the effect is what happened. Sometimes the effect is stated before the cause. Events or facts are presented with the outcomes or effects.	☐ So ☐ For this reason ☐ Accordingly ☐ Because ☐ Since ☐ Nevertheless ☐ Therefore	☐ If…then ☐ This led to ☐ Reason why ☐ As a result ☐ May be due to ☐ Effect of ☐ Consequently
Question/Answer	Question is presented which is followed by answers.	☐ How ☐ Who ☐ What ☐ One may conclude ☐ How many	☐ When ☐ Where ☐ It could be that ☐ The best estimate

What type of structure would be a best fit for a diary or science experiment? What about a book about whales or a book about the four seasons? Which text structure would be best for presenting information about weathering?

But WAIT, here's an important point to remember, which can make things just a bit more complicated for readers. Although one specific text structure will probably be dominant in a text, other structures may also be present in that text, as well. In other words, some texts may include more than one text structure so it is important that we help students learn to determine the primary text structure for a text. When readers are aware of text structures, they are likely to use more effective strategies for reading comprehension (Duke, 2014).

An effective tool for teaching text structure is through the use of graphic organizers, which visually represent the relationship among key ideas. Graphic organizers help the reader not only distinguish between text structures, but also help in organizing information for comprehension. Though they are helpful for all readers, graphic organizers can be particularly helpful for English language learners and struggling readers who can use these visual tools to help understand and organize the content. Now with the purpose of text structures and signal words associated with each, let's look further at how readers can gain deeper meaning of content through signal or summary questions and the use of graphic organizers.

Text Structure	Signal Questions or Summary Questions
Description	What person, place, thing, idea, event, or concept is being described? What are the most important attributes or characteristics presented?
Compare and Contrast	What is being compared? What characteristics are being compared? How are the items alike and different? What are common characteristics to both?
Sequence or Chronological	What are the major events that have taken place? What sequence of events is discussed in the text? How is the sequence of events presented in the text?
Problem/Solution	What is the problem(s) and why is it a problem? What are some possible solutions? Does the author present a best possible solution and state why?
Cause/Effect	What specific event has occurred? What was the cause(s) of the event? What was the effect(s) of the occurrence? What were the results or outcomes of the event? What was the significance of the event? How did the author detail the sequence of events and the relationship between cause and effect?
Question/Answer	How are the answers to questions presented? Is there enough information to adequately answer the question posed? What other information would help the reader? How thoroughly is the topic covered?

BECOMING FLUENT IN THE LANGUAGE OF CONTENT

Analytic Graphic Organizers for Text Structures

Before we look deeper into the use of graphic organizers, it is important to have an understanding of their origin and how learning theories apply to using them to benefit learners. Graphic organizers were primarily introduced by Richard Barron (1969) along with the term itself, but graphic organizers are rooted in the earlier work of Ausubel (1960; Manoli & Papadopoulou, 2012). Ausubel used the term "advance organizers" and according to his cognitive theory of meaningful learning, the use of organizers enhance learning by helping readers retain unfamiliar but meaningful information (Ausubel, 1960). He believed that new information is learned when it is linked to the learners' existing cognitive structure, which is consistent with the schema theory (Anderson & Pearson, 1984; Manoli & Papadopoulou, 2012).

According to schema theory, our mind is comprised of cognitive structures of knowledge "schema," which is background knowledge of the learner. When a learner takes in new information and integrates it with existing knowledge, learning is enhanced and new mental pockets are created to store the newly acquired knowledge. An important process in acquiring new information is the ability to organize the new concepts by building on and adjusting existing schema. Therefore, the purpose of a graphic organizer is to activate learners' prior knowledge and connect the new information to the previously stored information for meaningful learning to occur (Ausubel, 1960). For example, children may have knowledge or schema about a butterfly and maybe even a caterpillar,

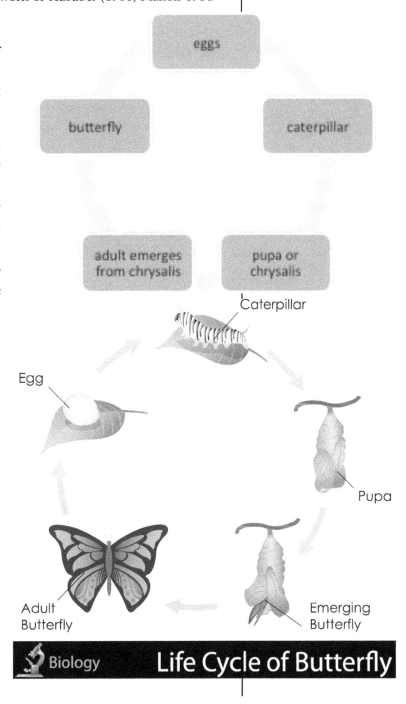

but do they have the knowledge that a caterpillar becomes a butterfly and it begins with an egg? The graphic organizers below are not complex, yet they show the lifecycle of a butterfly and provide new vocabulary for students in a visual representation.

Why use graphic organizers? Isn't this just filling in a bunch of bubbles arranged on a page? Graphic organizers are so much more than just putting information on a page; they guide learners' thinking as they fill in and construct a visual map or diagram with relevant information from a text. Because they help learners make connections and structure their thinking, graphic organizers provide some of the most effective learning strategies for readers and can be applied across the curriculum to increase learning and understanding of the language of content (Darch, Carnine, & Kameenuii, 1986; Manoli & Papadopoulou, 2012). They are communication devices that depict the structure of information and reduce the cognitive demands of the learner. Depending on the task, a variety of graphic organizers can be used as a visual display to facilitate learning of relationships between facts, concepts, or ideas within a broad topic.

In addition to helping learners organize their thinking and make meaning of new information, graphic organizers can serve as an instructional tool. Teachers can use graphic organizers to demonstrate how to organize information about a topic or text and though beneficial to all students, graphic organizers are powerful tools to help English language learners and students with language-based learning challenges make meaning of complex subject matter (Horton, Lovitt, & Bergerud, 1990; Manoli & Papadopoulou, 2012). Effective teachers guide students through the purpose and process of using graphic organizers because they know that students are more likely to learn the content at a much deeper level, making the information clear and meaningful. As students understand the content on a more complex level they become strategic learners, analyzing, thinking critically and creatively, communicating, constructing patterns of thinking, and ultimately making meaning.

Effective instruction in the use of graphic organizers involves a great deal more than just writing information in the bubbles or boxes provided on an organizer (Manoli & Papadopoulou, 2012). While this is where students record information when constructing a graphic organizer, most importantly is what occurs before and after the information is noted in the boxes. Before the information is put into graphic organizers, readers must use higher order thinking skills and engage in powerful information processing strategies such as using signals or cues to make decisions about what information is essential and consolidating that information, identifying the main ideas and supporting details, and determining text structure and the author's intent.

After the significant information has been recorded and organized into a graphic, a variety of instructional higher order thinking activities can be im-

BECOMING FLUENT IN THE LANGUAGE OF CONTENT

plemented. The organized information can help facilitate in-depth discussions; prioritize the information; and help learners elaborate, draw conclusions, make inferences or connections to other ideas, and extend understanding of important content (Darch et al., 1986; Manoli & Papadopoulou, 2012).

Teaching Students to Construct Graphic Organizers

So let's look at the steps to instructing students in the use of graphic organizers. The ultimate goal is for students to construct them individually; however, teachers must model and provide sufficient and effective instruction in *why* and *how* to complete a graphic organizer for comprehension of the subject matter (Horton et al., 1990). A well-developed graphic organizer will help students understand a network of information related to a central topic. So it is essential that teachers scaffold student learning through the construction process and use a gradual release process, moving from modeling to creating independently.

Step 1: The teacher models construction of a graphic organizer and conducts a think-aloud so students better understand the thinking process as information is selected to include in the graphic and other information is intentionally not included. This is very important when complex or new information is presented and a new text structure or graphic format is introduced.

Step 2: The class as a whole co-constructs the graphic organizer, making decisions as to what needs to be included and what is not as important. Also, students make decisions about where to record the information. The teacher facilitates the process.

Step 3: Small groups of students construct a graphic displaying the information they deem important in a way they can better understand the information. Students must negotiate what information to include and where to note it for organizational purposes. The teacher serves as a guide-on-the-side.

Step 4: Students construct their own graphic organizer in a way that helps them better understand the concept or subject. This process allows each student to individually create a visual organization that meets their personal needs as a learner.

Keeping Students Engaged

How do you keep students engaged in the use of graphic organizers and stimulate their use of them to enhance learning? This is a question that is often posed by teachers as students get uninterested in constructing graphic organizers on a continual basis. Keeping students motivated by providing many different ways of learning the content is excellent practice. As teachers, we must constantly strive to engage students and avoid the ever looming beast called *boredom!* Use a wide variety of graphic formats and continually move from whole group, to small group, to partner or independent practice based on the content and support students need. Sharing many possibilities of different ways to organize information provides new opportunities of conceptualizing information. For students to develop depth in understanding about a specific structure and graphic format, they need more than a one-time exposure to it. As with most other skills that are of value, effective modeling, guided practice, and multiple opportunities for independent practice are needed. Only then can students begin to internalize and effectively use the strategy.

As a general rule, most students need approximately 15 to 20 different meaningful experiences with a specific organizational structure before they really begin to understand and use it independently. With this being said, it is also important that teachers find a balance in providing so many different learning opportunities that the effectiveness of instruction is lost by including too many different strategies or graphic possibilities content (Darch et al., 1986; Manoli & Papadopoulou, 2012). There is often a thin line between sticking with a particular graphic organizer long enough for it to truly influence student learning and loosing student interest with the response, *"Do we have to create a graphic organizer again?"* Effective teachers communicate the purpose and goal for student learning of content and how important organizing information is to the process. It is a constant assessment and reflection process to monitor the pulse of the classroom to determine instructional approaches that will engage and stimulate student interest.

Assessing through Graphic Organizers

Graphic organizers can be a very powerful assessment tool to determine students' knowledge of the content or subject matter covered, their critical thinking skills, and their ability to organize and structure information (Horton et al., 1990). As students construct a graphic organizer, teachers can assess their understanding of the key concepts and how they interrelate by listening as students explain their graphic and how they determined the organization of and the information to include. Through observation, teachers are able to evaluate considerably more about the depth of comprehension and learning versus student completion of a pencil and paper test (Afflerbach, 2004). Teachers often choose to use a rubric to assess and evaluate the complexity of each student's graphic as an indicator of ability to organize and structure information as well as indices of creativity and quality. As you assess students and create a graphic organizer, think broadly. You will want to assess much more than just the outcome; as noted earlier in this section, it is important to be aware of and assess what happens before and after construction of the graphic organizer for each learner.

When creating graphic organizers for your students it is helpful to have a place for the students to record the signal words and/or summary questions to help them make connections to the text structure the author used and assist in organizing important information. You will find a variety of graphics at the end of this chapter for the various text structures. Here is an example of possible graphic organizers for each text structure. As you can see they do not have to be complex to begin with and students can expand the graphic to show the networking of concepts as their understanding evolves, making them as detailed as necessary for understanding. Another consideration is the level of the student and the topic of study.

Evaluating Nonfiction

One of the greatest challenges teachers have is selecting high-quality non-fiction when there is so much to choose from. There is not one book or text that will fit the needs of all readers. The varying topics, lengths, and levels of difficulty, as well as formats, makes it a monumental task at times, and as difficult as this is for teachers, our goal as educators is for students to become adept in the process. Therefore, we must have strategies to teach students to evaluate efficiently and one of the most effective is using the 5 *A*'s Moss (2003) presented when determining high-quality texts. The 5 *A*'s discussed below are a good method of evaluating a wide array of sources of nonfiction, as well as information accessed digitally.

1. *Authority* of the author—does the author note experts that were consulted and credit them in the text?
2. *Accuracy* of text—does the author state facts and theories? Is the text current and are the visual images clear?
3. *Appropriateness* of text for audience—is the information presented in a way that is appropriate for the intended audience?
4. Literary *artistry*—does the author use literacy devices to make the information engaging and help readers connect to the text? Is the style of writing appealing to readers?
5. *Attractiveness*—does the appearance and the format of the text invite readers?

This process needs to be modeled and a variety of texts used to demonstrate differences in texts and what constitutes high-quality nonfiction literature. Students need many opportunities to analyze and evaluate texts, as well as to discuss the "why" in their evaluative process. It would be good to have these 5 *A*'s posted in the classroom so students can refer to them often. Now that we have looked at ways to evaluate a text overall, let's consider how readers can determine accuracy of information.

How Do Readers Know if the Information Presented Is Accurate?

One of the most important aspects in determining high-quality nonfiction is dependent on the authors' knowledge about the topic and their ability to convey their expertise in the subject to the reader. The language the author uses, terms, explanations, and discussion are crucial to readers believing in the credibility of the author to write about a given subject. With so much information readily available, it is essential that readers become critical consumers of information and sources. Readers want to know that authors not only know the subject well, but that they have the ability to convey the information in a way that learners can understand complex information (Kristo & Bamford, 2004). There are several features in nonfiction that can help readers determine the accuracy of the information and the knowledge and expertise of the author (Kristo & Bamford, 2004).

- **Copyright date**: the date of publication indicates how current the information is

- **About the author:** this tells the author's background and provides the foundation of what the author knows or the level of experience with the subject—that is, the author's credentials
- **About the photographer or illustrator:** presents the credentials of the photographer or illustrator including how the artist created the visual images or was able to obtain the photos
- **Dust jacket:** the paper that wraps around a text can provide much information, including about the author, a summary of the content, or a brief story about the author or illustrator's experiences with the subject
- **Acknowledgements or dedication:** these often note who has contributed to the text and their level of expertise in the subject; it can also include organizations or institutions
- **Bibliography:** this helps readers determine currency of research and how extensive the research review was and what other relevant materials were explored
- **Preface and/or introduction:** the author provides an overview of the subject, a brief summary of what readers will find in the text
- **Specialized language:** author uses language related to the content and explains the terms in a way readers can understand
- **Epilogue or afterword:** provides a summary of the research, noting the strengths of the research and areas that may need further exploration

The bottom line is that readers must know how to determine the credibility and relevancy of the information in a text. Readers must learn to critically evaluate materials and not take what is presented at face value. As teachers we must guide students through the process of questioning sources and seeking specific information that helps determine the integrity of the author and the reliability of the information.

Text Features to Support Comprehension

So what are text features and how do they help readers to access information?

Now that you have a foundation of the various text structures, let's look at what features authors use to enhance their text and assist readers in gaining understanding of the content. The meaning of a text is not communicated merely by the printed words on a page, and this is especially true of nonfiction texts. Text features support comprehension by helping readers identify important information and understand challenging ideas (Duke, 2014). Text features are the building blocks for text structure. In essence, they are to nonfiction texts what story elements are to fiction. (As a reminder, you may refer back to the chart at the beginning of the chapter, which depicts the differences in genres.) The various features an author chooses to use help readers make sense of what they are reading and access information, which is very important in comprehension.

Text features and text structure go hand-in-hand to support comprehension of nonfiction texts. Comprehension could be seriously compromised without these to help readers determine what is important to the text and what is important to them as a reader. For example, without a table of contents, readers can spend a lot of time flipping through a book to find the specific information they need. Some other features that support comprehension are bolded words or specialized print, which helps draw the reader's attention to important or key words and phrases. Often the definitions of key words or vocabulary specific to the content are presented in a way that notes the importance of the vocabulary to the reader. Additionally, visual images such as maps can help the reader see where a geographical location is and put it into perspective with the reader's location while building understanding of various places in the world. Diagrams can help readers understand the anatomy of an animal through presentation of a detailed photograph with labels to support the reader's comprehension; and indexes help readers quickly locate specific information in the text.

Because text features are so important in understanding complex materials and subject matter, it is essential that the use and benefits of each feature be explicitly taught to students (Kelley & Clausen-Grace, 2010). Most often readers of all ages skip over the features and this is especially true for challenged readers who struggle with text in general, let alone add a lot of features on a page that looks extremely cluttered. Since this can be overwhelming for some readers, it is important to teach the purpose of each feature and how to access information important to understanding the content. You must explicitly point out each feature and the information it provides the reader students (Kelley & Clausen-Grace, 2010). Also, it is important to show readers the options to read through a nonfiction text.

Current nonfiction texts are highly visual, which provides great support for the young readers today as they live in an extremely visual world with everything at the touch of a finger. High-quality nonfiction provides visual aids and texts that complement each other, so all levels of readers can benefit from the information. Readers may read through the narrative expository passages first or choose to read the side bars, diagrams, charts, or other features first, then go back and read the discussion. It depends on what is beneficial to the reader in understanding the content. For instance, in a text about whales, it may benefit the reader to look at diagrams of the parts of whales and charts that depict similarities and differences of whales (compare and contrast graphics) before reading what the author has to say about whales in general. This builds background knowledge for the reader and provides visual images for comparison. However, other topics may benefit readers more by reading the narrative first and gaining an understanding of the topic overall and then use the access features to better understand the specific aspects of the subject matter. As a teacher you need to know the text and the reader so you can best determine the approach to the text. You must take some time to look through texts and make note of features, such as photographs/illustrations, sidebars, charts, graphs, or maps, to determine how students may benefit most from the text and features (Kelley & Clausen-Grace, 2010).

A strategy that may be beneficial is to show students how important text features can be to support learning, so you may intentionally skip over the text features when reading or cover the text features and have students read part of the text without them first. After doing so, reveal the features and discuss how they support understanding of content and how difficult comprehension was without the support. Then, reread the text with the features and discuss with students how much comprehension increases and how the specific features support learning of the content.

The following chart shows some common features in nonfiction and how they support readers with comprehension.

Feature	How It Supports the Reader
Table of contents	Helps readers identify key topics in a text and locate the topic quickly and efficiently
Glossary	Helps readers find definitions of words that are in the text and are important to understanding the content
Index	An alphabetical list of ideas that are in the text that helps readers locate what page the idea is on
Chapter or section headings	Informs readers of the overall topic to be presented
Subheadings or subtitles	Help readers to know specific topics or content-related information relative to the overall topic
Illustrations, sketches, or pictures	Help readers understand what something actually looks like and supports the narrative discussion
Diagrams, cutaways, cross sections	Help readers understand size relationships, how information is organized, cross sections or cutaways of deeper parts of a bigger picture, or a sequence of processes and cycles
Graphs	Some information cannot be presented in narrative form and must be presented as a visual; graphs can show changes over time in a line graph or show comparisons vertically on a bar graph
Labels and/or captions	Words or phrases that help readers identify specific features or parts of a picture or illustration, as well as learn vocabulary specific to the content
Charts and tables	Provide a visual display of important information organized in rows and columns with headings to categorize information and make comparisons

Maps	Help readers understand geographic locations and where they are in the world, as well as spatial relationships of size and distance between various places
Special print	Authors may bold, italicize, or underline important words to draw the reader's attention
Bulleted or numbered lists	Helps the reader note important points or steps without reading through a narrative to determine key ideas

Evaluating Text Features to Support Comprehension

For text features to truly be an effective tool for comprehension, students must have a firm understanding of what they are and how to use them to access information. This is more than just being aware of what a text feature is, it involves analyzing and evaluating the features to determine the purpose and function of each feature. It is helpful for students to first take a visual stroll through a text to see what type of features are included and use the following overarching questions to guide them in examining various text features before reading through the text.

- After looking at the text features presented, what type of information do you think you will find in the text?
- What do the text features tell you about the author's intentions and the structure of the text?
- How do the features organize information and help you find information?

This process will not only help readers understand the features included, but it will also help them determine if the text has the information needed that will assist them in understanding the concept or topic of study. Students need to be able to evaluate informational texts to select high-quality literature that presents current, accurate, and relevant information. By applying criteria to evaluate a text, students will develop a better understanding of how to select high-quality texts as well as how to maneuver through the features to support comprehension. This also allows students an opportunity to compare and contrast text structures and determine the features an author uses to present information.

So what does this process look like for students? To have students practice using criteria to evaluate informational texts, provide a wide array of nonfiction materials and have them work in groups to take a visual stroll through a text, focusing on only one feature at a time. After doing so, have them first respond to the three questions noted above. Then have the group of students select another text and respond to the questions on the chart below regarding the various text features included. The questions below will help guide students in evaluating text features. (In the instructional resources section you will find a copy of the following charts to help students to analyze informational texts.)

Text Feature Analysis

Analysis of Features	Included?	What would you suggest to make the text better for the reader?
Is the copyright date of the book recent so the information is current?	Y or N	
Is there information about the authors to help readers know their background and experience regarding the topic of the text to determine credibility of information? Are they qualified to write about the subject?	Y or N	
Does the table of contents provide an efficient way for readers to find information?	Y or N	
Are chapter titles included that will guide readers to specific categories of information?	Y or N	
Do chapters or sections have headings and subheadings to direct readers to specific topics?	Y or N	
Is there an index to guide readers to specific pages containing information they may be seeking?	Y or N	
Is there a glossary to help readers find definitions for specific vocabulary? Does it include a pronunciation guide to help readers learn how to say the words?	Y or N	
Is some information accentuated for readers by the use of different fonts, italicizing, bolded print, underlining, or bullets?	Y or N	
Are the graphics visually appealing and support understanding of the content?	Y or N	
Do the visual images have captions and explanations to support understanding of the graphic and the subject matter?	Y or N	
Is the information presented in parts so the content can be understood?	Y or N	
Does the style the author used to present the content make the topic and the text interesting and engaging?	Y or N	

Learning about Informational Text
Semantic Feature Analysis Chart

Things about Informational Text

Types	Organization	Access Features
Concept	Enumerative	Headings/subheadings
Photographic	Sequential	Sidebars
Survey	Chronological	Bulleted information
Reference	Question/answer	Insets
Specialized	Narrative	Easy to Navigate?
Other	Other	

Patricia Durham, 2011

BECOMING FLUENT IN THE LANGUAGE OF CONTENT:

As you can see by these questions, the process can be very thorough and help readers to consider the many aspects of text features and author style. By having readers note what could better support readers in understanding the content of a text, they look through a more critical lens in determining the quality of the text, as well as how to apply strategies readers use to learn the language of content. Once students become more adept in determining what constitutes high-quality nonfiction, they can use their knowledge of text features and text structures to comprehend the content or subject matter. They will have the support of new reading strategies to acquire information and build new schema.

Something to Think About!

With the vast amount of informational texts around us, developing the literacy skills of students is essential in becoming critical consumers of not only the information but the sources of information as well. Strategies needed for nonfiction are different than those needed when reading fiction. The reader must be aware of and use strategies to both access information and to build schema. Nonfiction texts that are well organized, current, engaging, and provide strong visual images and clear explanations support understanding the language of content. Authors' use of text structures and text features are central to helping readers gain access to information and organize it in a way they can understand the subject (creating those mental pockets). With such a wide array of nonfiction available, students need many opportunities to explore and evaluate a variety of materials. They are immersed in nonfiction on a daily basis in the world around them, so why not immerse them in the classroom as well? This needs to begin in the earliest of years and not become the focus in the upper grades and beyond. With skills and strategies to maneuver and understand informational materials in the earliest of years, we open the door to critical thinking, evaluating, and processing, which are essential for life-long learning.

"If uncovering the truth is the greatest challenge of nonfiction writing, it is also the greatest reward." —Candice Millard

Chapter Five

Designing Instruction through the Five Literacies

To map out a course of action and follow it to an end requires some of the same courage that a soldier needs. — Ralph Waldo Emerson

At this point, your Content Language Checklist is growing and even possibly overflowing resulting in the need for an additional copy (check the appendix for that!). Having a critical eye for strategies that develop content language fluency *and* to expose students to multiple text types creates authentic learning experiences. These experiences help students become fluent in the language of content and critical consumers of information. This chapter provides various approaches to designing instruction with the focus of mapping out content language strategies over the course of a unit of inquiry. Your Content Language Checklist will be a valuable reference for designing lessons that build fluency in the content language.

DESIGNING

Standards will tell you the learning expectations for a unit of inquiry, but what expectations will you have for them to become consumers of that content? When thinking about the design of a unit of study, consider these questions:

- How do I want my students to navigate through the content?
- How will I facilitate students manipulating the content to become fluent readers, writers, speakers, thinkers, and listeners?
- How do I want students to sound when speaking about the content?
- What do I want students to take away from reading the content?

- Why will I have students write about the content?
- How will I design the unit to foster engaged thinking of the content?
- What can I do to create opportunities for students to be active listeners?

Planning and designing requires a road map for getting to the big picture—that is, becoming fluent and critical consumers of knowledge. To build a point of reference for crafting lessons using the elements of the five literacies, let's take a look at how a simulated third-grade unit of inquiry on ecosystems is mapped out over the course of eight instructional days to help students become fluent consumers of that content (see chart, Unit of Inquiry—Ecosystems Third Grade).

(A) observe and describe the physical characteristics of environments and how they support populations and communities within an ecosystem;

(B) identify and describe the flow of energy in a food chain and predict how changes in a food chain affect the ecosystem such as removal of frogs from a pond or bees from a field; and

UNIT OF INQUIRY—ECOSYSTEMS THIRD GRADE

	Main Content Language Objective	Frontloading	Content Manipulation	Backloading
Day 1	Speaking/Listening/ Thinking	Puzzler/Unlock the Door	Visual Content Language Maps	Think-Pair-Share
Day 2	Speaking/Listening/ Thinking/Reading	I Think, I Know	Feature Scavenger Hunt/ Stop-Drop-Draw	Visual Content Language Maps (Revisited from Day 1)
Days 3-4	Speaking/Listening/ Thinking/Reading	Unlock the Door Revisited (Day 3) I Think, I Know (Day 4)	Text Set Exploration/ Discover Circles with Multiple Text Types	One-Minute Quick Write and Think-Pair-Share (Day 4)
Day 5	Speaking/Listening/ Thinking/Reading/ Writing/Viewing*	Agree/Disagree	Visual Manipulation of the Content/ Media Viewing	Agree/Disagree
Days 6-7	Speaking/ Listening/ Thinking/Writing/ Viewing*	Unlock the Door Final (Day 7)	Internet Workshop/ Digital Media Viewing/ Three-Minute Quick Speech	
Day 8			Summative Assessment	

Designing Units of Inquiry

The third-grade student expectations for this unit of inquiry are to observe and describe the symbiotic and interconnectedness of organisms and environments (see sidebar on state standards). Designing units of inquiry creates a classroom environment that allows learners to interact, engage, and manipulate content knowledge while fundamentally satisfying a natural curiosity to uncover the elements of the unit (Kristo & Bamford, 2004). This inquiry can be a few days, or extend across a whole grading period of one to three weeks. Within a unit, all five literacies can be vehicles for learners to critically consume knowledge. Through this design you are developing content language fluency as learners engage with the spoken, heard, read, written, and viewed* aspects of literacy while critically thinking about the content knowledge.

DAY 1

On the first day of a unit of inquiry the main objective is to activate background knowledge, establish a vision for the inquiry, and to build motivation for the students to want to be engaged learners during the following days of the unit. In chapter 2, you were introduced to several content language developing strategies such as the Puzzler, Unlock the Door, Agree/Disagree, Visual Content Language Maps, and Think-Pair-Share. Notice in the unit inquiry chart how those strategies support each other over the course of a week and can be interchanged as Frontloading and Backloading strategies. The beauty of such strategies is the authentic nature to engage students in active thinking, listening, and speaking. These are opportunities for students to use their schema to confirm prior understanding but also for that prior understanding to be put to the test and extended through academic curiosity. For example, the Agree/Disagree strategy will let students contemplate their thoughts and opinions regarding the ecosystem based on their background knowledge or their educated "hunch." Throughout the week, students confirm their opinion, change it, or evolve it based on your teaching (refer to chapter 2 for review). Day 1 content literacy strategies capitalize on these opportunities to build intrigue and motivation at the start of the unit. It also allows students to have input on their learning vision.

---

*Viewing as a literacy—Viewing is related to creating and interpreting images (pictures, charts, graphs, maps, videos).

Unit of Inquiry—Ecosystem Frontloading/Backloading Elaboration

Puzzler and 'I Think/I Know' Concepts for Ecosystem Inquiry
- Ecosystems
- Community
- Population
- Habitat

Small Group Visual Content Language Maps
- Desert
- Ocean
- Pond
- Forest

Agree/Disagree for Day 5 Media viewing
1. If a population leaves a habitat, it could cause problems for the ecosystems.
2. If humans need it, then it's always okay to take it from the Earth.
3. Nature needs a clean environment to keep habitats populated.
4. Sometimes too much of a good think can be bad.
5. All life in a community needs to work together.
6. Populations stay in the same place no matter what the environment is like.

VISUAL CONTENT LANGUAGE MAP

While this can be an individual activity on a single sheet of white paper, it can also be a great team building activity. Using large chart paper, have students do this same activity but as a mural. (See sidebar for group concepts to illustrate.) After time to illustrate has been given, students share their mural with the class owning their prior knowledge for this soon-to-be-explored ecosystem (refer to chapter 2 for an example that supports the ecosystem unit of ecology). What authentic classroom art and anchor charts you now have as reference!

Content Manipulation—Designing Instruction to Engage with Multiple Text Types

DAY 2

Beginning each day with a follow-up to a previous frontloading activity draws on the students' initial investment into the inquiry study, as well as continue to build momentum and commitment to unlock the mysteries of the unit of inquiry. Now that intrigue and vision have been set, Day 2 starts the process of finding answers to the curiosities established on Day 1 by manipulating content and being engaged with multiple forms of content text. Having preselected terms that will help build the language of the content, Day 2 begins by engaging in the "I Think, I Know" strategy (refer to sidebar for key concepts to consider for the Day 2 frontloading "I Think, I Know" activity as well as chapter 2 for a refresher on procedures for the strategy).

Textbook section on ecosystems

TEXT STRUCTURE AND FEATURE SCAVENGER HUNTS

In *Preparing Teachers for a Changing World: What teachers should learn and be able to do* (2005) it is discussed that too often it is assumed that because students <u>can</u> read, they know <u>how</u> to read all text types, or because they are struggling readers they are not capable of navigating through the text. It is also discussed that success in becoming fluent in content language—specifically becoming a fluent reader of informational text—is reliant on navigation tools students have in their learning toolbox to manipulate text in an engaging way. Therefore, students need the opportunity to become familiar with the language structure of a given content, be it oral or written, as learning content subject matter is analogous to learning a second language. Furthermore, it is dangerous to assume that either they should be *able* to read text or they are *incapable* of reading text based on language observations (Valdes, Bunch, Snow, Lee, & Matos, 2005). In chapter 4, you explored nonfiction through a critical lens looking at text structure and how to best help your students navigate nonfiction. The chart, Before Reading Strategies, from chapter 3 of this book presented a variety of before-reading strategies you can equip students with to navigate nonfiction, one being "noticing structure of the text." While many high-quality texts are available for students, the traditional textbook type of informational text is one that students will encounter throughout their grade school lives and into their college years. Valdes and colleagues (2005) agree that we as teachers do students a useful service by offering experiences to navigate texts like these. With that said, there needs to be structure and support to guide students through effective engagement with text. Chapter 4 then introduced you to the many aspects of nonfiction text structure as well as the variety of features nonfiction authors use to assist readers to navigate their text. Let's take a closer look at Day 2 and how students can manipulate content using a traditional science textbook section.

The **Feature Scavenger Hunt** noted in Day 2 of the unit chart offers the reader an opportunity to become familiar with the text by investigating the structure and author's intent for reading the selection (refer to chapter 4 for review of text features). It offers students a before-reading opportunity to explore the

---

FEATURE SCAVENGER HUNT

Directions: Use the assigned pages to locate the information below.

1. Locate 6 information captions. (Visual Information: Labels and Captions)
   Which one has the most interesting fact? Why?

2. ____ Locate 4 side bars. (Access Feature)
   Which one do you like best and why?

3. ____ Find 2 titles. (Access Feature)
   ____ Find 8 subtitles. (Access Feature)
   What do you think you will read about based on the titles and subtitles?

4. ____ Find 1 diagram. (Visual Information: Diagrams)

5. ____ How many vocabulary words are boldfaced? (Style of Writing: Vocabulary)
   Which word is most interesting? Why?

6. ____ Find 8 photographs. (Visual Information)
   Which 2 pictures do you like best and why?

7. Which feature did you find the most helpful and interesting?

Let's add this to the Content Language Acquisition Framework chart! What can you check off for its active engagement in building content fluency?

text features and make predictions. Many times, the sidebars and charts can go unnoticed by a reader or are not used to the fullest potential because often readers view informational text as only being found in the paragraphs that house the words. During the Feature Scavenger Hunt, students interact with challenging bolded vocabulary words, explore the visuals, and take note of the organization of the text—all before they even begin the actual reading process. Having this knowledge of the text upfront creates a road map for the student to use during the reading process. Take a moment to examine the example found in "Feature Scavenger Hunt for Ecosystems" and how it assists in previewing organizational structures and access features found in the reading of the textbook selection on ecosystems (see Textbook section on ecosystems).

To prepare for a **Feature Scavenger Hunt**:

- Explore ahead of time the features provided by the author.
- Decide what attention you want to give to certain features such as bolded words, captions for pictures, graphics, photos, or other aspects of the text that will benefit the reader.
- Create a scavenger list for the reader to use during prereading.
- Go over the list in small groups or in class.

Stop-Drop-Draw. Additionally in Chapter 4, you were presented with guidelines for teaching students to construct graphics. Tools such as these give a content language reader another tool to put in their toolbox for the during-reading process. After an activity such as the Feature Scavenger Hunt, which sets the motivation and expectation for reading the text, a student is now better prepared to engage with the text. Reading informational text requires a different approach than reading fiction. The text is dense with content information and a higher text complexity level due to the vocabulary that is unique to the language of the content. Students might find this more manageable by "chunking" and processing smaller parts of the text rather than trying to engage with it in one long read. Using a self-made graphic organizer like "Stop-Drop-Draw" is not only useful for the current reading task, but is transferable to future, more independent engagements with multiple text types. Below are some guidelines for conducting a "Stop-Drop-Draw" during-reading strategy:

- Prior to reading, determine 3-7 stopping places for the selected reading.
- Using plain white paper, fold into quarters and number each box appropriate to the amount of planned stopping places. Make sure the last box is empty. The back can be used if more than 5-7 stops are planned.
- When demonstrating this for students, model what the words "Stop... Drop... and Draw" mean. Explain that you will STOP orally and visually following along with the text, DROP a page holder and close the

> Let's add this to the Content Language Acquisition Framework chart! What can you check off for its active engagement in building content fluency?

BECOMING FLUENT IN THE LANGUAGE OF CONTENT

book (can turn the page over if not a book), and DRAW the first image that might be important to remember related to the selected reading.

- Teacher begins reading the first selection.
- When the first stopping point arrives, call out "Now, Stop… Drop … and Draw!" allowing time for students to draw.

Stop Drop and Draw stop #1

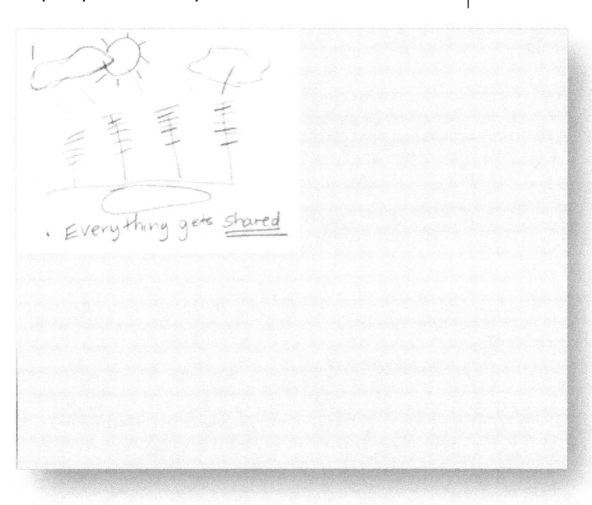

- Provide time for students to Think-Pair-Share with the person sitting next to them. Once the pair has both shared, guide the students to write one "take-away" statement in the box (see Box 1).
- Call for pairs to share with the class either what they personally discussed or something that they heard being discussed.
- Continue the procedure until all sections have been read and discussed (see Boxes 2 and 3).
- After the last section has been read and discussed, ask students to use the last empty box to write a "repeat worthy" statement about the whole selection that they might share with someone when asked… "So, what did you learn at school today?"

Stop Drop and Draw graphic

Stopping point #2

BECOMING FLUENT IN THE LANGUAGE OF CONTENT

This self-made graphic organizer becomes a summary of the reading as well as a resource for reviewing for any summative assessment on the content. You might offer to allow this to be used for the first few minutes of an assessment. It builds "buy-in" for the strategy for a student to know that the time invested into completing a graphic organizer was worth it later in the unit of inquiry. There may need to be more scaffolding the first few times this strategy is down in class, but over time and with release of control the students take away a new tool for their learning toolbox!

As a backloading activity to Day 2, notice in the unit plan that after new content has been manipulated, students should return back to the murals of Day 1 and as a group define and label using the key concepts from the "I Think, I Know" activity (refer to chapter 2 for an ecosystems example). As always, scaffold this experience with language by guiding them using one concept word at a time, and then listen to all that authentic content language being used!

Text Set Exploration and Discovery Circles

DAYS 3-4

You have now found yourself about halfway through the hypothetical unit of inquiry, and deep in the content! Students have been interacting and manipulating the language of ecosystems while building a deeper schema to support independent learning. Take this opportunity to visually measure how much students have been learning by revisiting the Unlock the Door strategy done on Day 1. Move "keys" into the keyhole that students feel have been discussed and learned. Make a mental observation of what is still left to uncover during this unit of inquiry. Use the question keys still outside the keyhole to access the direction of the unit. Will these questions be addressed during the remainder of the unit? Remember, some may not be addressed based on the nature of your focus of inquiry and might be considered for independent student inquiry at the end of the unit. For Day 4, you might revisit the "I think, I know" strategy and find that you begin to hear students move away from "I THINK that means" to confidently stating they "KNOW" the understanding of the concepts. After visiting the

THOUGHTS ON WHOLE CLASS READING

Many educators have learned that the classroom practice of students taking turns reading aloud in a content textbook is problematic. Activities such as these are called Round Robin reading or Popcorn reading. Students were called on to read and turns basically went around the classroom reading a paragraph at a time. What tended to happen here was a student being traumatized to read aloud in front of the whole class or would count which paragraph he/she would be assigned to read. Most students were found to read ahead to practice and not really engage with the rest of the text. In Popcorn reading students might be randomly selected to read so to "keep them on their toes." You may very well recall instances like these. This type of reading does not have a place in a classroom! In chapter 3, we pointed out how important it was to match informational text with the reader when students are reading independently. In most situations, whole class oral reading of a text will not match all students' reading levels; therefore, student oral reading should only be done in a guided reading small group where the focus might be on how to guide the reader to lift the text off the page rather than how to navigate and organize the content knowledge.

When modeling how to navigate through text or utilizing graphic organizers with a text as a whole class... YOU be the reader of the text. Students then are able to focus on the tool and get experiences with developing the *listening* aspect of literacy!

> **TIP:** Remember the importance of modeling the process! Refer to the Chapter 6 section, "Modeling the Process of Exploration and Discovery."
>
> **TIP:** Make sure the Learning about Informational Text chart is modified if using digital text.

> Let's add this to the Content Language Acquisition Framework chart! What can you check off for its active engagement in building content fluency?

frontloading strategies, it's now time for this unit to become more student-led in their inquiry through a Text Set coordinated with Discovery Learning Circles. Quality guided inquiry takes more time, so consider allocating multiple days.

TEXT SET EXPLORATION

In chapter 3 (pages 50-52) we laid out a framework for creating worthy text sets. Having used this as a guide, you might have worked with the librarian as well as personally collected a variety of informational text pieces that represent an array of nonfiction types. Remember the importance of a variety of text pieces, including digital. Chapter 7 provides you with a variety of resources to locate quality pieces of digital text using an eReader or tablet (refer to the section, "Using a Critical Lens for Selecting Digital Media"). While this will be a great addition to the classroom library, for today, the students are going to work in groups and explore the printed texts to become familiar with the collection you worked hard to create. Think of a **Text Set Exploration** as the "movie trailer" for your text set. It will help promote and display the pieces for future independent student selection. With the collection of text pieces for the text set, divide among predetermined grouped students, maybe two to three pieces per group. After introducing each piece of the Text Set to the class, these pieces rotate around the room using a set time length so that all students can become more aware of the pieces. Similar to the **Feature Scavenger Hunt**, a Text Set Exploration guides students to becoming familiar with the organizational structure and type of informational piece, which can better prepare for navigating independent reading (review Chapter 4, "Text Structures and Signal Words"). Using a tool such as the "Learning about Informational Text" chart, students working as a group select a piece and begin to explore for such attributes as:

- What type of organizational structure does the piece have?
- What type of text would it fall under?
- What are some basic access features?
- What purpose might I read the piece for? Academic or personal?

As a team, the students judge and analyze to check off qualities found in the piece. Once again, step back and listen! Listen to the language of informational text being exchanged and challenged among the students. Brookhart (2010) describes quality teaching that supports higher level thinking skills as teaching that assists students to transfer their learning into other contexts and provides problem-solving situations for students to discuss, debate, provide rationale, and reflect on decisions. Such experiences lead to developing higher order thinking skills. Having students explore texts using the foundational knowledge of

BECOMING FLUENT IN THE LANGUAGE OF CONTENT

informational text structures leads to becoming critical thinkers of texts and analyze what it has to offer them as a reader and consumer of that content. As Duke (2004) would agree, not only have they previewed the structure of texts, but through the experience you created they have developed authentic opinions on texts that might enhance the inquiry of the content.

Discovery Learning Circles. With a variety of texts on ecosystems explored, students have a good foundation to move into independent reading of texts. Chapter 6 presented a detailed explanation of the benefits implementing Discovery Learning Circles has to offer for your students. Take this implementation seriously and pace your class to Discovery Learning Circles. Guidelines such as those found the textbox under "Writing and Recording Information Discovered" will be helpful when conducting Discovery Learning Circles for the first time. While Discovery Learning Circles offer a variety of ways to use texts for inquiry, the students' personal choice caters to their personal motivation for inquiry. Managing the Discovery Learning Circles for Day 4 while also offering personal choice is not as daunting as it sounds. Below are some suggestions to narrow the selections:

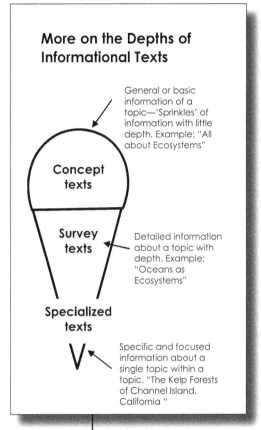

More on the Depths of Informational Texts

General or basic information of a topic—'Sprinkles' of information with little depth. Example: "All about Ecosystems"

Concept texts

Survey texts

Detailed information about a topic with depth. Example: "Oceans as Ecosystems"

Specialized texts

Specific and focused information about a single topic within a topic. "The Kelp Forests of Channel Island, California "

- Let the students in each group decide on a piece (even the selection to read from it!) to use for Discovery Circles.
- Have students star the top three choices from the Learning about Informational Text chart.
- Collect the chart on Day 3 and examine for possible grouping while taking into account readability and interest.

Remember for a short reading session, keep the length of text manageable by selecting a section of pages from the text that can be read in one sitting by the students. Employ several of the strategies offered in Chapter 6 for writing or recording information from text, such as Post-It with Purpose, Journal Entries, Coding the Text, Word Cluster Boxes, and Semantic Feature Analysis charts.

Backloading with a One-Minute Quick Writes. Asking students to compile the information in a formal product (Chapters 9 and 10) should be done with proper structure and guidance, but there are a variety of informal sharing opportunities that can be done allowing students to cash in on the effort of learning about a content and sharing it with an audience. Following Discovery Circles, One-Minute Quick Writes coupled with Think-Pair-Share offers students the chance to demonstrate such learning. Just as the name suggests, provide students with a time of one minute to write down, bullet out, or draw and label what they have come to understand about the unit of inquiry

Let's add this to the Content Language Acquisition Framework chart! What can you check off for its active engagement in building content fluency?

Learning about Informational Text
Semantic Feature Analysis Chart

Book Title

Qualities of Informational Text

Types
- Concept
- Photographic
- Survey
- Reference
- Specialized
- other

Organization
- Enumerative
- Sequential
- Chronological
- Question/answer
- Narrative
- other

Access Features
- Headings/subheadings
- Sidebars
- Bulleted information
- Insets
- Easy to Navigate?

BECOMING FLUENT IN THE LANGUAGE OF CONTENT

through Discovery Circles (in this scenario it would be regarding ecosystems). The only catch to this strategy is that they must be engaged with the task for the full one minute. Some suggestions to offer for staying engaged if students find they have exhausted their knowledge base: Rewrite, rephrase, and/or add detail drawing. When time is up, have students share their writing in a Think-Pair-Share (refresher on this can be found in Chapter 2!).

Visual Manipulation of Multiple Text Types— Media and Digital

DAY 5

Viewing media has many possibilities in the content classrooms. Critiquing commercials, examining websites, watching movies, and even using videos as a mentor text type offer students an opportunity to develop the skills of finding the authors'/directors' purpose or hidden messages as well as to apply skills as critical consumers of knowledge, to compare and contrast valid opinions, possible propaganda, and learned content within a given context (refer to Chapter 7 regarding developing digital literacies). There are places in our classrooms for all of these and more. Take, for example, the simple task of viewing a movie.

> Make a connection with the Visual Content Language Map done on Day 1 by having students illustrate the setting of *The Lorax*. In a class discussion, have students identity the ecosystem, community, population, and habitat.

Movies and videos are a great way to show students that the content they are learning can be used in other forms outside of the classroom. If designing a media viewing day like the one planned for Day 5, teachers can frontload the experience with an opportunity for the students to go into the viewing session with something that will guide the experience and assist them in comparing and challenging their understanding. Keeping with our ecology unit of inquiry, a teacher can frontload the viewing of *The Lorax* (1973) with the strategy Agree/Disagree (see Chapter 2 for procedures and the sidebar found in this chapter by Day 1 for examples of Agree/Disagree statements). After the viewing, students return to the statements and reevaluate their opinion discussing why they either still hold their original opinions or have changed their position.

Buehl (2006) points out that it is necessary for teachers to provide structure for students to differentiate between what is interesting to them and what is important (or the academic take-away) from the text but also to make connections between both those domains. He suggests providing a simple graphic organizer during the viewing of text such as the one below to assist students in this task. By simply trifolding a sheet of paper, students can track their interaction with multiply text types and use as a source for discussion. It can be paired with a frontloading strategy such as described above or used as a standalone.

Graphic Organizer for Viewing Media

What is interesting to me?	What is important for learning?	What is both interesting and important?

TIP: Since students will be using information gathered for more than the day of the unit, it might be helpful for there to be a storing or retaining procedure in place such as a folder.

DAYS 6-7

As this unit of inquiry is coming to a close, it is time for students to bring together all the knowledge acquired. What better way to bring this to an end than to return to what started it all by revisiting the Unlock the Door poster. Led by the students, move keys into the keyhole that they feel have been addressed. With what is left unanswered, you can assign independent inquiry. Take this time to reflect on the activities engaged with throughout the unit. It is now time for students to bring all the documents together for a celebration of knowledge. Students will need their visual content language maps (both from Day 1 and from the media viewing), the Stop, Drop, and Draw graphic organizer, the Learning about Informational Text chart, the notes from Discovery Circles, the One-Minute Quick Writes, and any other notes/sheets that was asked of them during the unit (yes, even traditional worksheets!). While they have been engaging in multiple literacies throughout the unit, Days 6-7 will have students manipulating the content language through spoken literacy.

Mentor Speech via Digital Media. In Chapter 1, the importance of providing a communicative purpose for learning content was discussed so students can negotiate understanding and have an authentic environment for using the language (refer to "Speaking" in Chapter 1). If we as teachers want students to be authentic speakers of the content, we also need to expose them to what that sounds like. Mentor speakers are valuable for showing students what it sounds like to be a speaker who has been successful at delivering a message. Spoiler alert for novice teachers: I am sad to say this, but for most situations we really are not those mentors. Many students just don't see us in that role, and that is okay for there are plenty of mentor speakers available at your fingertips just like there are plenty of mentor texts available on your bookshelves. Students need to see themselves in the mentor speakers they study. They need to connect technique and style with someone they can relate with personally. Two great examples of such mentor speakers are Robby Novak who is known for playing Kid President and Emma Watson aka Hermione Granger in the *Harry Potter* film series. Robby Novak would be a great mentor for younger grades and Emma Watson for older. Take a moment and watch the two videos and take note of what you notice about the delivery. (See appendix for full transcript of Emma Watson's HeForShe speech.)

> Watch Emma Watson at https://www.youtube.com/watch?v=oE28bb11GQs
>
> Watch Robby Novak as Kid President at https://www.youtube.com/watch?v=4z7gDsSKU-mU&list=PLzvRx_johoA-Yabl6F-WcU-jL6nKA1Um-t&index=15

As presented in Chapter 8, Internet Workshop can be a valuable platform for studying mentor speakers. Using a YouTube mentor speaker video such as Kid President, the teacher begins by conducting a Think Aloud to study various delivery mechanics. Delivery mechanics in a speech might be considered similarly to author's craft and purpose in Readers or Writer's workshop. Possible delivery mechanics include the following:

- Intonation
- Pacing and pausing
- Mannerisms
- Body language
- Verbal emphasis
- Eye contact
- Structure of the speech
- Language use
- Mode of delivery

Following the Think Aloud, students are invited by the teacher to participate and experiment in a type of Interactive or Shared Speech, practicing with the teacher-highlighted delivery techniques of the studied speaker video. With some guidance behind them, students move to working individually or in pairs during the next part of an Internet Workshop—Independent Speech writing time. During this time, students have the opportunity to begin crafting and practicing a speech that is inspired by the mentor speaker. In the unit of inquiry designed in this chapter, two days are allotted for exploring new delivery mechanics to experiment within their own speeches on ecosystems. For students to fully be in an Internet workshop platform, tablets or computers would need to be accessible so they can retrieve and reference the mentor speaker being studied while they are crafting their speech.

For many students, speaking in front of peers is frightening even with a well-crafted speech. Offering short-time limits can help with this, and having catchy titles such as, "The Amazing Two-Minute Speech," can make it less daunting. Two minutes? No problem! Anyone can talk for just two minutes! And it is amazing just how much can be said.

Something to Think About!

Crossing Standards. Step back and look at how much designing a unit of instruction such as this can be accomplished to assist students in becoming fluent in the language of content! Reading, writing, speaking, thinking, and listening can be interwoven throughout the unit leading to engaged and critical learning. Bunch and colleagues (2005) explain that "they [teachers] must examine how their particular disciplines (math, science, social studies) use language, and they must become aware that ways of speaking and writing in these disciplines—in addition to the specialized vocabulary used in the discipline—make particular demands on students." This is exactly what is meant by reenvisioning your role as a content language teacher. Yes, it can be done! Even if you are wondering about finding time and resources, it can be done with the acceptance that you are indeed a content "literacy" teacher responsible for designing instruction that moves the content beyond the facts and helping students manipulate the content using the five literacies. If you are a self-contained teacher, one way to find this time is to integrate with the language arts block. If you are a departmentalized teacher, here is your invitation to team teach and collaborate with the language arts teacher to become more efficient with the time allotted. Look at the literacy skills embedded in the unit of inquiry designed during this chapter in the textbox, "Crossing Standards with Third Grade Literacy Standards." Use this or similar standards as a means for collaborating across the curriculum and forming relationships with your counterparts within the school. Owning your identity as a content language teacher opens up possibilities in teaching that can positively impact the perspective your students develop for becoming fluent content language users beyond your classroom! As Ralph Waldo Emerson said at the beginning of this chapter, it only requires the courage to envision the design!

Design is a funny word. Some people think design means how it looks. But of course, if you dig deeper, it's really how it works.

—Steve Jobs

BECOMING FLUENT IN THE LANGUAGE OF CONTENT

Crossing Content Standards with Third-Grade Literacy Standards

(2) Reading/Beginning Reading/Strategies. Students comprehend a variety of texts drawing on useful strategies as needed. Students are expected to:

(A) use ideas (e.g., illustrations, titles, topic sentences, key words, and foreshadowing clues) to make and confirm predictions;

(B) ask relevant questions, seek clarification, and locate facts and details about stories and other texts and support answers with evidence from text; and

(C) establish purpose for reading selected texts and monitor comprehension, making corrections and adjustments when that understanding breaks down (e.g., identifying clues, using background knowledge, generating questions, re-reading a portion aloud).

(3) Reading/Fluency. Students read grade-level text with fluency and comprehension. Students are expected to read aloud grade-level appropriate text with fluency (rate, accuracy, expression, appropriate phrasing) and comprehension

(9) Reading/Comprehension of Literary Text/ Literary Nonfiction. Students understand, make inferences and draw conclusions about the varied structural patterns and features of literary nonfiction and respond by providing evidence from text to support their understanding. Students are expected to explain the difference in point of view between a biography and autobiography.

(11) Reading/Comprehension of Text/Independent Reading. Students read independently for sustained periods of time and produce evidence of their reading. Students are expected to read independently for a sustained period of time and paraphrase what the reading was about, maintaining meaning and logical order (e.g., generate a reading log or journal; participate in book talks).

(13) Reading/Comprehension of Informational Text/Expository Text. Students analyze, make inferences and draw conclusions about expository text and provide evidence from text to support their understanding. Students are expected to:

(A) identify the details or facts that support the main idea;

(B) draw conclusions from the facts presented in text and support those assertions with textual evidence;

(C) identify explicit cause and effect relationships among ideas in texts; and

(D) use text features (e.g., bold print, captions, key words, italics) to locate information and make and verify predictions about contents of text.

(14) Reading/Comprehension of Informational Text/Persuasive Text. Students analyze, make inferences and draw conclusions about persuasive text and provide evidence from text to support their analysis. Students are expected to identify what the author is trying to persuade the reader to think or do.

(16) Reading/Media Literacy. Students use comprehension skills to analyze how words, images, graphics, and sounds work together in various forms to impact meaning. Students will continue to apply earlier standards with greater depth in increasingly more complex texts. Students are expected to:

(A) understand how communication changes when moving from one genre of media to another;

(B) explain how various design techniques used in media influence the message (e.g., shape, color, sound); and

(C) compare various written conventions used for digital media (e.g., language in an informal e-mail vs. language in a web-based news article).

Crossing Content Standards with Third-Grade Literacy Standards (cont.)	
(20) Writing/Expository and Procedural Texts. Students write expository and procedural or work-related texts to communicate ideas and information to specific audiences for specific purposes. Students are expected to: (A) create brief compositions that: (i) establish a central idea in a topic sentence; (ii) include supporting sentences with simple facts, details, and explanations; and (iii) contain a concluding statement. (B) write letters whose language is tailored to the audience and purpose (e.g., a thank you note to a friend) and that use appropriate conventions (e.g., date, salutation, closing); and (C) write responses to literary or expository texts that demonstrate an understanding of the text. (21) Writing/Persuasive Texts. Students write persuasive texts to influence the attitudes or actions of a specific audience on specific issues. Students are expected to write persuasive essays for appropriate audiences that establish a position and use supporting details. (28) Research/Organizing and Presenting Ideas. Students organize and present their ideas and information according to the purpose of the research and their audience. Students are expected to draw conclusions through a brief written explanation and create a works-cited page from notes, including the author, title, publisher, and publication year for each source used.	(29) Listening and Speaking/Listening. Students use comprehension skills to listen attentively to others in formal and informal settings. Students continue to apply earlier standards with greater complexity. Students are expected to: (A) listen attentively to speakers, ask relevant questions, and make pertinent comments; and (B) follow, restate, and give oral instructions that involve a series of related sequences of action. (30) Listening and Speaking/Speaking. Students speak clearly and to the point, using the conventions of language. Students continue to apply earlier standards with greater complexity. Students are expected to speak coherently about the topic under discussion, employing eye contact, speaking rate, volume, enunciation, and the conventions of language to communicate ideas effectively. (31) Listening and Speaking/Teamwork. Students work productively with others in teams. Students continue to apply earlier standards with greater complexity. Students are expected to participate in teacher- and student-led discussions by posing and answering questions with appropriate detail and by providing suggestions that build upon the ideas of others.

SECTION III

Designing Instruction to Support Content Language Acquisition

Chapter Six

Acquiring the Language of Content through Discovery Learning Circles

"Discovery consists of looking at the same thing as everyone else and thinking something different."
— Albert Szent-Györgyi

For many years the traditional approach to teaching content area subject matter was dominated by teacher-centered instruction, with emphasis on textbook reading and the occasional inclusion of supplemental videos or outside resources. Sound familiar? Not too effective in learning the language of content or subject matter, as the teacher generally did all of the talking and students listened, then took a test. Today's learners are not so tolerant of learning environments that lack engagement and interaction. Learners of today bring a whole new level to the terms "visual" and "auditory" learner as they are constantly connected to friends, family, and technology. With this in mind, let's look at how the five literacies apply to learning the language of content through concept discovery learning circles. As you read through this chapter keep in mind the five literacies to make connections to the purpose and process of discovery learning circles. We hope you will see how the format of the discussion circles intertwine the five literacies throughout the process, as well as contribute to the significance of engagement and collaborative learning.

When students have a better understanding of how to evaluate and maneuver through nonfiction text, they are ready to investigate and explore text and materials, discovering new information and content vocabulary. We now want to provide them opportunities to "give it a go" and practice what they know about reading and writing nonfiction through discovery discussion groups. Through participation in discovery learning circles students are provided rich opportunities to read, write, speak, think, and listen about content while acquiring a new and deeper understanding of the subject matter under study. But, before we begin, let's look at the concept and principles of discovery learning and how they apply to the purpose and process of concept discovery learning circles.

Discovery Learning

Bruner (1967) introduced discovery learning as a method of inquiry-based instruction. His outline of the principles of discovery learning are similar to the theories of Dewey (1916) and Piaget (1954), in which both believe that discovery learning includes learners as active participants in the learning process through exploration, questioning, seeking answers, and developing more questions. Learners are provided opportunities to build on past experiences and knowledge, while using their imagination, intuition, and creativity. Students search for new information to discover important facts, make correlations, and find new truths. Learning does not equal absorbing what was said or read; learning is actively seeking for answers and solutions.

Bruner (1961) believed the following in regard to learning and education:

- Curriculum should support the development of problem-solving skills through the processes of inquiry and discovery.
- Curriculum should be designed so that the learner experiences mastery of skills which lead to the mastery of other, more in-depth skills.
- Subject matter should be presented in ways to connect to a child's way of viewing the world.
- Teaching includes organizing by concepts and learning through discovery.
- Culture should shape thinking through which people organize their understandings of themselves and others, along with the world in which they live.

In discovery learning, the role of the teacher is to facilitate the learning process by providing opportunities for learners to have access to new content and concepts, yet allowing the learner to organize the information in their own mental pockets. Through discovery learning, students build on prior knowledge through experiences and searching for new information and relationships based on individual interests. In essence, learners are constructing their own meaning as they make sense of information. Bruner's (1961) Discovery Learning Model integrates five principles:

- **Principle 1: Problem Solving**
  Teachers should guide students to seek new information and search for answers or ways to solve problems. The learner is the driving force

and teachers should motivate and encourage risk taking, probing, and critical thinking.

- **Principle 2: Learner Management**
  Teachers should provide opportunities for students to work in groups, with partners, and independently. Additionally, it is important that students learn at their own pace and that the learning process is flexible, which is far different than the traditional lesson cycle with a static sequence of activities and planned implementation and outcome.

- **Principle 3: Integrating and Connecting**
  Teachers facilitate learners in combining prior knowledge with new information and encourage them to make connections to the real world. This encourages learners to extend what they know and discover something new.

- **Principle 4: Information Analysis and Interpretation**
  Discovery learning is process oriented, in which students learn to analyze and interpret newly acquired information that includes far more critical thinking and creates deeper levels of understanding.

- **Principle 5: Failure and Feedback**
  Learning does not occur when learners find the right answers; it also transpires through failure. Discovery learning does not place emphasis on finding the end result, but it focuses on the new things discovered throughout the process. It is important that teachers provide feedback along the way so learning will be more complete.

The methods implemented in the Discovery Learning Model can vary based on purpose and the needs of the learner; however, the goal is always the same, for learners to reach the end result on their own. Through exploration, questioning, examining, making connections, and manipulating situations, learners are more likely to understand new concepts and retain higher levels of newly acquired knowledge. So let's look at how the principles of discovery learning are applied in content discovery learning circles.

Purpose and Planning: Content Discovery Learning Circles

Content discovery learning circles provide a way for students to work in small groups to explore, discuss, dig deeper for meaning, organize information, and apply the skills and strategies needed for understanding of content and make personal meaning of texts. Discovery learning circles encourage authentic, student-centered discussions and interactions versus the teacher-directed question /answer instructional approach (Kristo

& Bamford, 2004). This concept may seem similar to the literature circles process, which is often included as a component of the literacy program in many classrooms, yet they are different in many ways. Like literature circles, discovery learning circles are small, student-led discussion groups; however, group members may have a copy of the same book or text to read or they may have different texts, but on the same topic to explore and discover new information. Additionally, each member may assume a specific role with responsibilities to contribute to group discussions or they might just have open-ended conversations about what they are reading and make connections to vocabulary and other information that other members are sharing.

The circle concept provides a way to engage all group members in a discussion of a topic and content under study while simultaneously allowing them to develop literacy skills and strategies with informational texts. Learning can be scaffolded as group members co-construct meaning of new information through discussion and exploration of materials. Concepts or topics may be presented by the teacher to support science or social studies content or students may be given choice and voice in selecting topics of personal interest to explore and discover. So let's think about what this might look like and sound like.

Consider a group of second-grade students exploring and discovering information about life cycles of animals as they search through a variety of materials. What might students discover? Maybe they will learn that most animals, such as reptiles, fish, birds, and mammals, have very simple life cycles: they are born, either alive from their mother or hatched from an egg and then they grow up. There are three stages: pre-birth, early life, and adulthood. They look like their parents, just smaller. What vocabulary might students acquire? How might they compare animals as they explore?

Now think about the discussion students might have when they discover information about animals that undergo metamorphosis, such as frogs, newts, or butterflies. These animals undergo huge changes from the way they enter the world. For example, a frog lives the first part of its life underwater breathing through gills and the later part of its life breathing with lungs and has the ability to live on land or underwater. Or what about a caterpillar that wraps in a cocoon and emerges a beautiful, colorful butterfly that is exceptional in design. These animals have a unique "wow factor" as they experience major changes from birth to adulthood. So what vocabulary might students discover with these types of animals? What dialogue might they develop? What are some questions they might have? What do you as the teacher want students to take away from the discovery and discussion process?

BECOMING FLUENT IN THE LANGUAGE OF CONTENT

Unique Features of Content Discovery Learning Circles:

- Students lead discussion of content discovery
- Small groups of 3–6 students, depending on the subject matter
- Students may be assigned a topic or a group at times
- Students may be given voice and choice at times for topics/groups
- Students may take on roles to facilitate the discussion process
- Students can evaluate texts and information together
- Students take notes about the readings and share with group
- Many types of nonfiction materials may be included for discovery of content
- All members may have the same text or each member may have a different text, but on the same topic
- Discussions include information about content under study, but also how they accessed information (the process)
- Discussion of text structures and features are included in the circles
- Teacher may provide guided instruction in the group to teach strategies or skills, as well as help integrate and connect new information
- Teacher assesses discussions and notes information discussed, as well as areas that learning needs to be extended

There are important considerations so each student will benefit from the collaborative discovery process. Discovery learning circles should be fairly small, between three and six members, to provide optimal opportunities for students to engage in the process of investigation and discussion. Students may be grouped by interest or in groups with varying reading levels to support one another as they work together to learn the language of content. Look at the various ways to implement discovery learning circles in your classroom. As you will see it depends on the purpose of the circle process and the goal for student learning.

The Role of the Teacher and the Role of the Learner

When teachers include content discovery learning circles as an instructional approach, they are sharing control of the class with students. Often teachers are not comfortable relinquishing power and decision making; however it is essential for the process to be effective. In discovery learning circles as in literature circles, the teacher provides modeling and guidance to support student learning. However, in content discovery learning circles, the teacher's role of modeling and guiding students in the various types or levels of discovery learning is essential for students to access and discover new information.

Discovery learning circles allow for appropriate integration of the five literacies in content areas, as students apply reading and communication skills to learn more about various subject matter and communicate their understandings or questions about the text to peers. Principle 2 of the Discovery Learning Model (Learner Management) directly applies to the group format where the majority of the discussion is generated among the students, with the teacher monitoring from the background. Students take ownership of the mission and content, yet at times teachers provide guided reading lessons prior to discovery learning circles or throughout the discussion circle process so content acquisition will be more meaningful and also to increase the likelihood that students will transfer their reading knowledge to other reading situations.

As noted in Principle 3 (Integrating and Connecting), teachers help students integrate and connect new information, encouraging students to access prior knowledge and extend with newly acquired information. Teachers serve as facilitators or guides on the side, listening to conversations in discovery learning circles, making note of important concepts, vocabulary, and ideas that students discuss. Importantly, teachers also make note of concepts, ideas, and vocabulary that are ignored in order to pose open-ended questions in the follow-up large-group discussion to extend student thinking. The teacher assesses comprehension through questioning but does not model or teach students how to understand the text. Remember Principle 1 involves problem solving, allowing students to probe, explore, question, and construct knowledge. Now think about Principles 4 and 5 in the model—as students analyze and interpret information they are discovering new content. The importance of this process is the discovery along the way, not just the search for a final answer. The role of the teacher in extending thinking and providing feedback at various times in the discovery process is essential to student learning.

As students participate in concept discovery learning circle discussions, they are taking ownership of their own learning, changing the typical interactions of content area subject matter, and contributing to making content learning more engaging and interesting. Students are explorers, investigators, readers, recorders, listeners, thinkers, and ultimately learners as they move fluidly through various roles in the process. Additionally, as students participate in small, student-led discussions, they are experiencing democratic social interaction, which will help them become successful members of society by engaging in discussions about significant concepts and ideas with peers.

Modeling the Process of Exploration and Discovery

The process of concept discovery learning circles doesn't just happen, it must be presented, explained, and modeled by the teacher. The teacher may present skills or strategies in exploring various nonfiction texts while "thinking aloud," modeling the thought processes needed to explore and learn new information. There are also different levels and purposes in discovery learning circles. A most effective strategy to learn the procedures is for a small group of students to participate in a "fish bowl" discovery learning circle with the teacher serving as the facilitator, while the rest of the class gathers around and observes the process. This can help students grasp the process of exploring and discovery, as well as sharing what they are finding in the materials. New vocabulary can be discussed and connections to personal experiences and the real world can be made. Look at the titles listed that may be included in a mini text set of books about bats, appropriate reading levels for second and third grade. Place these texts in the middle of a content discovery learning circle group and model the process of exploring and sharing your discoveries both about the texts and the content. Note how the process might look and sound in the box below.

- *National Geographic Readers: Bats*, by Elizabeth Carney
- *Bats! (Time for Kids Science Scoops)*, by Nicole Iorio
- *Zipping, Zapping, Zooming Bats*, by Ann Earle
- *Bats*, by Gail Gibbons
- *Bats (Nocturnal Animals)*, by Angelique Johnson and Gail Saunders-Smith
- *Stokes Beginner's Guide to Bats*, by Kim Williams and Rob Miles
- *Bats—Creatures of the Night*, by Joyce Milton

Place several texts about bats in the middle of the circle to explore, then select one to peruse, thinking aloud for students to hear your thought processes, *"I am going to look through the text titled,* Bats! (Time for Kids Science Scoops). *I wonder what information is in this text about bats? What features might it have that will help me find information?* Flip through the text and then stop at the table of contents. *This seems to be a descriptive text structure because the table of contents provides a list of topics that tell me where I can find information on different things about bats and the chapter titles indicate that they will provide descriptive information. For example, the first chapter is,* Bat Basics, *so I know I am going to find out some basic need-to-know information about bats in general. There are four chapters in this book and two sections at the end titled, "Did You Know" and "Words to Know." I think these will help me with new vocabulary about bats and give me some good answers to questions I might have.* As you flip through the text point out features. *I see some diagrams to help me understand the parts of a bat. Oh look, there are specialized vocabulary words in bold print and they are included in a side bar, as well. Hmmm…look at this word* (show students) *"echolocation." I can break this word into two parts because I know the words* echo *and* location *and I know what an echo is and what location means, so I wonder what these two words mean when put together? Now let's read the definition of this word. {Echolocation is the use of sound waves and echoes to determine location of an object. Bats use echolocation to send out sound waves from their mouth or nose to navigate and find food in the dark. It helps them find insects and mosquitoes.}* Make connections to other things when possible. *You know, now that I think about it I remember reading that dolphins have this same ability. I wonder what other animals might be able to use echolocation to find food or objects around them? I think I am going to put a sticky note here so I can come back to this question later. Let me look further in this text and see what other features might help me with new information.* Continue to point out various features and note how you are discovering new information. *Now, let's have each of you select a book or resource and see what you find out about bats.*

As the students explore and discover, encourage them to have open conversations about the new information they come across and share images, vocabulary, facts, and other pertinent information about the topic at hand. These grand conversations of discovery provide the foundation for new schema while connecting prior knowledge. Given the opportunity to explore and share their findings, students will be engaged in the discovery process and drive their own learning.

Students work in groups to sift through texts individually or with partners, then discuss their findings with all group members. Texts and materials selected can be any length and from many different sources, digital or print, as long as it is a useful resource to learn about the topic or content being studied and it stimulates meaningful discussion. As student are discovering, they write down important pieces of information and vocabulary to share with the group. After the discussion, students can combine what they discovered and choose what and how they want to demonstrate and share what they have learned. When students choose from many different materials with the purpose of coordinating and applying new knowledge, critical thinking is developed and learning occurs.

In content discovery learning circles, dialogue should include not only the content under study, but also how to read and understand the content using a variety of materials. As students interact with each other, they should be encouraged to share the process of discovery and the strategies they used to gain knowledge, such as any difficult words or definitions that posed problems, or concepts, ideas, and content that were challenging or unclear, and what they found helpful that led to understanding of the content. It can be music to a teacher's ears when they hear exchanges of conversations, such as: "Hey, I read that word too and didn't know what it meant. So I looked in the glossary and I think it means…what do you think it means?" or "Look at this diagram of a spider, now I can see where the eyes are and how many body parts they have. Did you know…?" This is what it means when students are developing language of content and content fluency as noted in chapter 1.

Guiding Students in Strategies for In-depth Discovery

Discovery learning circles can be challenging, encouraging critical thinking and moving beyond the surface meanings or simple interpretations described in a text. We want students to begin to question the *why* and *how* about topics or events. One of the strengths of discovery learning circles is that they can be used as a powerful teaching and learning strategy. Teachers can "step in" and "step out" as a guide to provide needed connections or strategies to help students gain access to new information and comprehend the content.

For example, a teacher may observe students asking superficial questions or not clearly explaining important vocabulary terms they discover in a text versus participating in genuine discussion, supporting higher levels of thinking among the group members. This is a great opportunity for a teacher to "step in" and prompt deeper discussion by asking some higher level questions to get students thinking and looking for information.

> For example, a teacher may observe students just talking about pictures of birds and identifying the ones with which they are familiar. So the teacher may "step in" the circle and ask what they are discovering and prompt some deeper exploration: "What have you noticed about some of the birds you have read about? What are some similarities? How do some differ?" Teachers may guide students to discover that some birds have wings and some don't or some fly and some don't. It is also good practice to just prompt with comments students have made: "I heard Isabella say that she noticed penguins had very funny shaped bodies and short legs and then Ethan said he thought that an ostrich had really long legs and big bodies. So you are wondering about their unique look. How can you find out more about them and their special features?" Through gentle guidance and scaffolding, students will make connections and develop their own line of questioning. This should be a seamless process and the teacher can "step out" as soon as students begin digging deeper.

By providing more guidance in the process and purpose of the circle and by clarifying the ultimate goal of encouraging thoughtful discussion about important ideas in the texts, students will be more successful in using the language of content, which leads to understanding of new content. It is essential that teachers monitor groups carefully to confirm they are having genuine discussions about important vocabulary and concepts. Additionally, students need to take notes and record new terminology and significant information throughout the circle discussions. The discovery process is not strictly about reading and discussing content subject matter, it also includes a process of recording what is being learned, questions that arise, or wonderings they may have that prompt further inquiry and reading. Then students will work as a group to organize what they have written and learned to gain a better understanding.

Teachers must model and guide students in finding themes and making connections, and students need opportunities to explore, but nonfiction materials are complex; therefore, the teacher should make use of instructional opportunities to make the circle process meaningful. As students practice and become more adept with the discovery learning circle process they will become more self-sufficient, productive, and rely on group members for understanding (Kristo & Bamford, 2004). The teacher can then step back and watch the development of learning and assess what students understand and where they need more support.

Evaluating Texts and Information

Discovery learning circles provide opportunities for students to critique the credibility of various sources of information. In the circle format, students can discover more than just content. With the many sources available, students can search for evidence that the authors conducted research and demonstrate they have knowledge of the content, note the sources used, and identify the authors' purpose in writing the texts. Students can compare information from various sources to verify the information is accurate and current. This includes features in the texts, such as illustrations, charts, tables, and diagrams to determine the consistency of the information as reported from several authors. Then students can weigh this evidence to decide if the text is a credible interpretation or representation of the topic under study.

Discovery learning circles can also offer the opportunity for teachers to teach strategies by encouraging students to recognize different perspectives on a variety of topics, historical or current. Even in the early primary grades students can distinguish that many authors provide different points of view on the same topic in their texts. Also important in determining the credibility of the author and text is for students to understand the differences in primary and secondary sources. This can be an important part of the discovery learning circle discussion process. When looking at various texts, students need to be able to determine that a primary source is a document or object written or created during the time under study. Primary sources were present during an event, experience, or time period and provide readers an exclusive view of a particular event, whereas a secondary source provides an analysis and interpretation of a primary source. Secondary sources are removed from the event by one or more steps and at times include pictures, graphics, or quotes from primary sources in them.

Roles and Responsibilities in Discovery Learning Circles

Literature circles are not a new concept in classroom practice. Teachers have used them as a strategy for students to read and discuss various novels and texts since they were introduced in the early 1990s by Harvey Daniels (1994). However, the process is a bit different when using nonfiction materials as students need strategies to understand the complexities of text structures, dense academic vocabulary, purpose, and multifaceted text features. Discovery learning circles can be confusing and unproductive if students do not know the purpose or the process. Lack of direction can result in students floundering with the task at hand; however, if they each assume a specific role with a responsibility to the group, a more successful process will unfold.

As a way of helping students become accustomed to preparing for and participating in discovery learning circles, students may be asked to be responsible for a specific role. By taking on a role in the group, students may be more productive and fruitful in gaining understanding of content as the roles will guide their reading and discovery. This also gives students voice and choice in the discovery learning circle process, as they can select a role that best suits their interest or skills and abilities.

Through roles in discovery learning circles, students are challenged to dig deeper in a text than they might if they read independently for a class discussion. Fulfilling various roles and responsibilities requires students to inquire and examine concepts and ideas more thoughtful to complete their task, then engage in thoughtful discussions with group members, presenting information about the concepts and ideas gained through completion of their role. In the discovery circle discussion process, students must be active participants in their learning by contributing to the group discussion, asking and answering questions, and thinking critically. As students accomplish their discovery circle roles, they must think deeper about the text and content to make connections between the text and self, text to text, and to the world around them. Additionally, learners integrate the five literacies as they engage in dialogue of new vocabulary and significant information about the content, and illustrate important aspects of the text or content for group discussion. This allows them to become fluent speakers of the content language.

Some roles can be similar to those used in literature circles and when reading fiction texts (Daniels, 2002); however, new and different roles are necessary for nonfiction reading and within the context of discovery learning circles (McCall, 2010). Roles can and need to be modified based on the text, topic, or genre being studied. Let's look at some possibilities for roles and the responsibilities that go with each.

Discovery Learning Circle Roles and Responsibilities

Role	Responsibility
Text Feature Director	The role is to guide the group in a stroll through the various texts, leading a discussion of the features in the materials as group members identify similarities and differences among the features. They can make note of specific features of a text on a sticky note and place on the front cover for group members to refer back to at a later time.
Real World Connector	The role is to make connections between events, ideas, people, or things presented in the readings and link it to their life, other texts, or the world around them.
Vocabulary Translator or Interpreter	The role is to identify and interpret meaning of new vocabulary terms that are important, interesting, puzzling, or unfamiliar to group members. They should also make connections to other vocabulary terms that students may know.
Investigative Reporter	The role is to locate specific information or sections in the text to help students understand the main concept of the readings or characteristics of people, events, animals, events, or things. They also seek answers to broad questions generated by the group before reading.
Question Generator and Recorder	The role is to generate questions and also record the questions of group members for exploration during the reading and discussion. They also record questions that arise throughout the discovery learning circle discussion.
Graphic Designer or Web Master	The role is to create a visual image of the information from the readings (a picture, graphic organizer, table, diagram, or flowchart or other image) to organize the content and help the group to develop a deeper understanding.
Historian	The role is to look at past events or people and find historical connections or reasons why an event occurred and the impact it had on others and future events.

Biographer	The role is to locate biographical information about important people in relation to the topic under study and share interesting facts with the group.
Social/ Cultural Connector	The role is to identify how an event or circumstance influenced groups of people, cultures, values of the time period, and society. They are to determine social and cultural connections that influenced history.

Writing and Recording Information Discovered

As students participate in discovery learning circles they have rich and rigorous conversations about a specific topic or subject matter; however, it is also important that they make connections through writing and recording of important information. If students stay deeply connected to the text and content, they develop habits for generating evidentiary arguments both conversationally and in writing to comprehend the topic under study. Students are acquiring new academic vocabulary that they need to access complex information, and through reading, writing, speaking, and listening they have strategic opportunities to practice use of common terms about a specific and, at times, challenging subject matter. Therefore, we need to guide them and model the roles and responsibilities that will help them become fluent in the language of content.

When implementing discovery learning circles it is a good idea to preselect four or five roles to introduce the job and the responsibilities that go with it each week at the beginning of the school year. The teacher models the job and all students in the group have this same job as they learn the duties of the role. Each week a new job is added, following the same format of introducing the new role each week, teacher demonstrates and models the role, then students practice the job throughout the week. At the end of four or five weeks, the students have a clear expectation as to what each role is and the responsibilities to the discovery learning circle group. This then transfers to each group member taking on different roles after they have applied what they have learned about each role. If you do this at the beginning of the year, then students will know what is expected when they meet in groups and you do not have to worry about this the rest of the year. It should become a well-oiled machine as students participate in groups throughout the year. You may choose to add a new role periodically, but it is important to follow the same process so students always have a clear understanding of the job before it is included into the discovery learning circle.

Emphasis on writing must be included as part of the discovery learning process, as students should include evidence to inform or share a perspective rather than the personal narrative format of reporting what they have read. Although narratives still have an important role, students strengthen critical thinking and writing skills with nonfiction texts by lifting important information from a text and recording it in various ways. This could include written arguments that respond to events, ideas, concepts, facts, and perspectives presented in the texts they read.

But in order to effectively determine important information, students must be taught strategies to decide what is important and how to record it for future purposes. Note-taking is a strategy that helps students become more effective in identifying important information, synthesizing, and comprehending content. As discussed in chapter 4, graphic organizers are one way to organize and record information specific to a particular text and note-taking is another way to assist students in understanding the content of their reading.

Also important is that students learn a variety of ways to access and record information. They need a lot strategies in their tool box to make meaning of nonfiction texts. There is not a one-size-fits-all text and topic strategy. Providing students with a variety of good note-taking strategies can afford them powerful skills as they progress through their education. The ability and need to take concise and effective notes is lost on many students. This process must be scaffolded from modeling a note-taking strategy to guiding students, then providing opportunities for independent practice. Although students often complain about taking notes on their reading, if presented with purpose and intent, and if set forth as an expectation for students, they will see the value. So let's look at some strategies that students may use when discovering and recording information that they feel is significant about a topic, then we will look at some possibilities for organizing the information.

Strategies for Writing or Recording Information from Nonfiction Texts

Reading comprehension instruction in the content areas includes strategies for tackling certain skills, like new vocabulary, identification of main ideas, and making comparisons within and between texts. What makes comprehension such a complex process is that understanding what anyone is reading is a completely personal and for the most part an internal task. In discovery learning circles students discuss their ideas after they've read something, but to track reading comprehension further, writing down thoughts and making connections demonstrates a deeper level of understanding. Comprehension of a text, especially more complex text, is comprised of smaller pieces, all of which must network in perfect harmony: an individual's background knowledge, vocabulary, or content language acquisition; his or her interest in the topic; and the individual's ability to make inferences and conclusions are all required—as well as many other skills. So it is important that students record information and their thoughts about the content as they are participating in discovery learning. This deepens understanding and provides students with a point of reference for future learning and discussions. Here are just a few ways that students can record information throughout their circle discussions. You may practice this as well by jotting down any ideas you have on the lines in the side bar as you read through the following approaches.

Post-It with Purpose: Post-it notes are far more than just a practical tool, they are simple and efficient sticky notes that can serve numerous purposes. In chapter 2, you were introduced to the concept of using Post-its with the whole-lesson strategy type activity "Sticky-Note Discussions." But in this context we will discuss some potential ways for using them in marking and recording important information in texts or as a quick way to jot down questions or ideas. The benefit to sticky notes is that they are easy to use and come in many sizes and colors, thus expanding the use to a variety of strategies. However, caution should be noted when introducing them to students, as they will overuse them by placing a note on every page unless you model and reinforce the fact that when they "post-it" they need to have "purpose." Let's look at some possibilities for student use in writing and responding to texts:

- Post a one- or two-sentence summary at the end of each section or page read.
- Record questions while reading or "on the spot" thinking.
- Jot down notes as groups jigsaw reading of one text to explore the content in general or jigsaw by reading from different texts related to the topic, but each explore one aspect, then share notes with the group.
- Take a gallery walk: Have questions posted around the room on chart paper and students respond on a post-it after reading and place on the chart.
- Then they can post further questions they have or respond to the questions of others.
- Use different colors of post-its for vocabulary, main idea, questions, AHAs.
- Write key words from the readings to include on a word wall.

- Using different color post-it notes, students work with a partner—one to find similarities about a thing, object, event or idea and the other to note differences.
- Write opinion or thoughts about a topic and then create a chart as a group and organize the views of the group by responses.
- Jot down quick notes to later expand and post in a journal.
- Respond to evidence-based questions while reading, placing a sticky note on the answer.

> Let's add this to the Content Language Acquisition Framework chart! What can you check off for its active engagement in build content fluency?

Journal Entries: Journals are beneficial across the curriculum as they are a place where thoughts are recorded and stored. This form of reflective writing helps readers develop their thinking. In addition to strengthening students' critical thinking skills, journal writing serves other purposes as well. Many teachers find that drawing or writing in a journal helps students to process ideas, formulate questions, and better retain information. Journal writing makes thinking and learning visible by providing a safe space for students to record thoughts and share feelings and uncertainties. In some instances journals may serve as an assessment tool, something teachers can read and review to better understand what their students know, what content or ideas they are struggling to understand, and how their thinking has transformed over time. By introducing a range of reflective approaches to journal writing, students generalize and connect their thoughts and beliefs about a topic or concept. Think of it as every student having a reflective lid and when you lift the lid you can see inside the container or pot, peaking into the metacognitive soup of students' insights, perceptions, attitudes, and views. There are many forms of journal writing that can be effective—the possibilities are extensive—but here are a few ideas to get you thinking:

- Scientific reflection: "Today I observed... I predict ... I also measured... I concluded ..."
- Three-column entry: Column 1—what I read, Column 2—my thoughts about the reading, Column 3—connections and experiences that connect to the reading
- Coding the journal: placing a star by statements that are most significant, question mark where you may need to go back and explain more, or highlight something that you want to explore further
- Write a letter to a historical character or write journal entries from the character or individual's perspective
- Draw pictures of an experiment and explain each step you observed
- Two-column entry: write about key ideas and then respond with personal thoughts

At times students may need some questions to initiate thinking about a new topic or concept. These need to be open ended so students can decide the direction. Here are some possible journal prompts to get students thinking:

Let's add this to the Content Language Acquisition Framework chart! What can you check off for its active engagement in build content fluency?

- What do you know about the topic before getting started and what do you want to learn?
- What "wonderings" did you have before and what "wonderings" do you have after reading and discussing?
- What information intrigued or surprised you?
- What is the most interesting thing you read or discussed?
- How can this information apply in your life or the world around you?
- What information did you or your group question or think might be inaccurate? Did the group or a group member check it out?
- What is the most important thing you have learned? Why?
- What techniques does the author use to make this information easy for you and/or the group to understand?

Coding the Text: This strategy directly supports discussion of the content in a discovery learning circle by providing students with text codes to note when they make connections to the reading. By writing specific codes that relate to their thinking and understanding while they are reading a text, students can then go back and discuss anything that was clear, unclear, or somewhat muddy with the group. This strategy can also include the use of post-it notes or the text may be something they can lightly record their code within a text using a pencil to directly write on an article or reproducible material. Students are provided a list of possible codes and they may use some or all of the text codes when reading. When a student comes across information that relates to one of the codes, they write the symbol next to the text or place a post-it note with the symbol. After the students have coded their texts, they can discuss and compare their codes with the group to gain further insight and listen to the thoughts and interpretations of others. It is a good idea to have the text codes displayed in the classroom so students can readily refer to them if necessary.

Let's add this to the Content Language Acquisition Framework chart! What can you check off for its active engagement in build content fluency?

Text Codes

Code or Symbol	What I Am Thinking
✓	This is something I know and understand.
?	I'm not sure I understand this. I need some more information or clarification.
+	This is important information! It is key or vital to the content.
X	This is different from what I know. It challenges my understanding and thinking.
!	This is exciting and surprising new information!
	I can see or visualize that! I made a connection!
	I made a text to text, text to self, or text to world connection.

Adapted from *Texts and Lessons for Content-Area Reading* by Harvey "Smokey" Daniels and Nancy Steineke, 2011

Reflecting through 1-2-3-4: After reading and discussing materials, students reflect on what they have learned about a topic by using this technique.

Write several sentences for each:

1. What is the big or main idea?
2. What are some personal connections you made?
3. What are some important details?
4. What are some questions you have?

Another possibility is to respond and reflect on three big questions:

1. What? What did you learn?
2. So what? Why or how is this relevant?
3. Now what? How does this apply or extend to other concepts or situations?

Word Cluster Boxes: Students may read different sections of a text and then discuss the reading or different texts on the same topic. As students read, they write down key words and concepts, building vocabulary or content language. Then students share their words and concepts as a group and make note of the ones that more than one student wrote down. Then the group decides which words they agree need to be written in the word cluster box as important to the content they are studying. This can be expanded as they continue the discovery process. Look at some possible words students may encounter as they read about the solar system and many more words can be added as students continue to discover.

Let's add this to the Content Language Acquisition Framework chart! What can you check off for its active engagement in build content fluency?

moon   stars   constellations
    sun   planets   orbit
comets   space   telescope
    solar system   planetarium
        lunar   eclipse
dwarf planets   asteroids

Semantic Feature Analysis: This strategy includes creating and organizing a grid to help learners explore how sets of things are related to one another. Learners look at specific information or features regarding a group of things, objects, ideas, and events; determine categories or characteristics to explore; then record the information located on a grid or chart. By investigating specific features, completing the grid, and analyzing the information, students are able to see connections, make predictions, and master essential concepts. Use of this strategy greatly enhances comprehension and vocabulary skills.

Look at the information presented in the chart below. As you can see this is a quick way for students to compare insects based on specific features. The final product of the feature analysis brings meaning to the subject matter, but remember this is at the end of the discovery process. So much learning has taken place along the way. This can be a way for students to pull the information together and sort out what they have discovered or this can also serve as a culminating piece to demonstrate what students have learned.

Insect	Characteristics				
	3 body parts	6 legs	has wings	bites	stings
wasp	X	X	X	--	X
bee	X	X	X	--	X
ant	X	X	--	X	X
mosquito	X	X	X	X	--
cricket	X	X	X	--	--
grass-hopper	X	X	X	--	--
beetle	X	X	X	Some types	--

Let's add this to the Content Language Acquisition Framework chart! What can you check off for its active engagement in build content fluency?

Sharing Group Discoveries

Follow-up whole-class discussions allow students opportunities to compare various perspectives about events or ideas and reasons for the interpretations and thoughts of classmates. This encourages and stimulates critical thinking about the diverse views of others regarding the same concept or subject matter. This is a crucial part of the discovery learning process—that is, sharing what students have learned.

Discussion of the content learned culminates with the group sharing their discoveries and knowledge with the class. The students should have the choice in how and what to present and there are a plethora of methods from which discussion groups may select—the possibilities are endless. Engagement and motivation are increased when students are empowered to have a voice in assignments and modes of presentation.

It is a good idea when you have groups with four or five jobs in each to have "like" jobs meet together with members from other groups. This will provide them an opportunity to share and compare notes and information to truly become the "expert" of the role. By delving deeper in cross-group discussions, but role specific, students collaborate and further their understanding through acquiring the language of content.

Look at the list below noting some potential culminating activities for students to present their discovery circle learning (Daniels, 2002; Schlick Noe & Johnson, 1999). As you read through these ideas, note others you have as they come to mind.

• Create a transcript of an interview of a person in the time period studied
• Create a map of a historical individual's journey, illustrating important settings, events, and tasks
• Write the ABC's of an event or information about a concept learned
• Complete a semantic feature analysis to show comparisons and organization of information
• Write a script for Reader's Theater and present to class
• Draw a diagram or other visual image to share
• Write journal entries from a historical person's point of view
• Conduct an experiment for the class
• Create digital presentations, including real photos or images and sound

Student Self-assessment—The Five P's: Preparation/Purpose/Participation/Process/Product

Reflection is one of the most important parts of the learning process. According to John Dewey, "We do not learn from experience … we learn from reflecting on experience." With this in mind we must provide opportunities for students to self-assess their own behaviors and participation in the discovery learning circle process and also to evaluate the effectiveness of the group as a whole. We want students to learn the content, but we must also nurture their social interaction and allow them to discuss what worked and what didn't so they can learn and grow. Here is an example of a rubric that students may complete based on reflection of their preparation and participation in the circle process. A copy of this can be located in the instructional resources section as well.

Content Discovery Learning Circle Self-Assessment/Group-Assessment and Reflection		Yes	No	Somewhat/ how to improve
Preparation	I completed all the required reading by the agreed on time.			
	My materials were prepared and detailed.			
My Role and responsibility	I completed my role and presented ideas clearly.			
	I used textual evidence to support my thinking.			
	I stayed on topic and was thorough in finding and presenting information.			
As a group member	I gave others the opportunity to participate and did not talk over others.			
	I listened thoughtfully as others shared their thoughts and information.			
Working together as a group	We worked together to make sure everyone participated.			
	We used respectful communication skills, only one person talked at a time.			
	We made sure each person provided evidence from the text.			
	We stayed focused and actively listened to each other and collaborated as we discussed the content.			
	All members were involved in the discussion and we encouraged each other to share.			

Group Assessment Reflection:

What was the most successful part of the discovery learning circle process?

What was the best thing about how your group worked together?

What was one problem that occurred in the group? How did the group solve the problem?

What should your group do next time to improve the discovery learning circle process?

What did you learn from the entire discovery learning circle process?

Something to Think About!

Content Discovery Learning Circles
Let's add this to the Content Language Acquisition Framework chart! What can you check off for its active engagement in build content fluency?

Through participation in content discovery learning circles, learners take on a leadership role and become directors in acquiring and internalizing knowledge, which translates into learning—not just temporary understanding or recall, but students truly learn the language of content.

Successful discovery learning circles allow for critical discussions about content, as well as incorporate the five literacies for students to make meaning of complex texts and content. Students will surprise you with profound questions and connections, along with thoughtful understanding. They just need opportunities to drive their learning, yet need you as their teacher, in a seat close by, ready to step in when direction is needed to keep them headed down the road of their learning journey.

"The real voyage of discovery consists not in seeking new landscapes, but in having new eyes." —Marcel Proust

SECTION IV

Digital Literacies and the Language of Content

$$E=MC^2$$

$$\pi = 3.14159265$$

$$V_f = V_i + at$$

$$a^2 + b^2 = c^2$$

$$H_2O$$

$$M = 5.9736 \times 1024 \, kg$$

2, 3, 5, 7, 11, 13, 17, 19, 23, 29, 31, 37, 41, 43, 47, 53, 59, 61, 67, 71, 73, 79, 83, 89, 97

Chapter Seven

Exploring Digital Literacies through a Critical Lens

If we marry educational technology with quality, enriching content, that's a circle of win.
—Levar Burton

The nature of literacy is changing as digital literacies evolve and enter our classrooms. The rate of growth of digital literacies has been increasingly rapid. No other technology for reading, writing, or communicating has been implemented so quickly, by so many individuals, in so many places, and with such broad consequences for literacy. So with this in mind, what do teachers need to understand about using the tools of digital literacies to promote the use and learning of content knowledge?

Extending beyond technical competence, the complex and transformative nature of digital literacies requires a careful consideration of how they influence and interact with the language of content and traditional print. In order to begin an examination of these connections, several aspects of digital literacies will be investigated: overall structure, defining features, diverse genres, and content for instructional purposes. Our focus with digital literacies and the content areas will be to answer these guiding questions: How is reading on the internet different from reading traditional print texts? What do teachers need to know and have access to in order to use digital literacies effectively?

Digital literacies include the language and literacy skills necessary to function in the virtual worlds of digital media. For clarity of understanding, several terms will now be defined before continuing in this chapter.

- **Digital**—digital information is stored using a series of ones and zeros. Computers are digital machines because they can only read information as on or off—that is, as 1 or 0. This system, called the binary system, can be used to represent incredible amounts of data which can easily be copied, moved, or changed.
- **Hybridity**—a mixture. In this case a mixture of genres or of traditional and digital texts.
- **Multimodal**—multiple sign systems, such as print-based and screen-based texts, primary sources (print and nonprint), video games, art, music, mathematics, graphic stories, graphic poems, performance poetry, animated narratives, comics, drama, drawing, portraiture, digital photos, claymation, tattoo designs, dance, audio books, picture books, e-books, and podcast and multimodal media production (Sanacore & Piro, 2014).
- **Monomodal**—using one method; in this case, possibly using only traditional books to access information on a topic.
- **Mash-up**—mixing context from various sources, such as combining a map with a graphic of age statistics or combining music from two or more recordings.
- **Media**—the means of communication: e-book, website, television, traditional book, etc.
- **Intertextuality**—the relationship between one or more texts in order to make meaning.

Structure

How are the literacy skills used with traditional print resources similar to and different from those skills used with digital technologies? Both offline and online approaches to literacy include accessing prior knowledge, inferential reasoning, and self-regulation. Researchers have noted that reading skills such as "selecting relevant passages and evaluating one's reading goal achievement," which are important when reading print, are *compulsory in hypertext reading*" (Coiro & Dobler, 2007, p. 242). Furthermore, while accessing background is a similar skill in both literacy approaches, in reading online, students connect with background knowledge on the topic and text structure they are investigating, but are also using background knowledge about websites and search engines. These four areas of accessing background information in online reading are examples of how digital reading is more complex than traditional print reading.

Let's think about another example that demonstrates how reading on the internet requires comprehension skills and strategies beyond those necessary to understand conventional printed texts: Text is interactive on the internet.

Readers actually define text structure in an online format by choosing links. Defining text structure creates many different possibilities for structure and content as individuals make personal choices of what to read. Furthermore, print literacy activities are usually designed by the author's defined structure, which is fixed. Online literacy events, however, can be accessed via different links, audio, video, and images creating dynamic documents.

Additionally, the depth and possibilities of online reading require readers to have strong organizational skills for comprehension of these multilayered online texts. The goals for reading a traditional print text and those for reading an interactive online text will likely be different (McEneaney, 2006). Additionally, three elements have been found to be an integral part of online reading: inferential reasoning, making predictions, and evaluating sources (Coiro & Dobler, 2007). While somewhat similar to traditional text reading, the inferences made during online reading are more complex and multidimensional. The predictions in internet reading are more numerous as each hyperlink is accessed, and the evaluation of sources becomes more necessary. All of these differences in online text structures and reading skills point to the importance of teachers' understanding the difference between offline and online reading. You may take a moment and refer back to the text structures discussed in chapter 2. Reflecting on the types of text structures of traditional texts may help you make connections to text structures in a broader sense as you read this chapter. What might you see as similarities and differences in traditional texts versus online texts?

Literacy activities in a conventional setting often include traditional print resources, but now the challenge for teachers and school districts is how to incorporate digital technologies within print-centric literacy programs (Walsh, 2010). To begin a discussion of the structure of digital literacies, it might be helpful to begin with a focus on organizational formats that are not productive. When media use is in the form of educational technology, such as canned video games and software (used repeatedly with little or no change), it does not have the same degree of challenge that commercial games do (Tyner, 2014). Students using the commercial games have more opportunities to interact and make decisions and may, therefore, be more motivated to engage in these games. Thus, the potential for meaning-making is embedded within these games. For digital literacies to have a transformative pedagogy, it is important for students and teachers to become involved in the multimodal, dynamic processes available in online spaces (Thomas, 2011).

View this video link, "What digital natives want from their libraries," and learn what young Abbey's digital literacy needs are:

https://www.youtube.com/watch?feature=player_embedded&v=7_zzPB-bXjWs

While very engaging, this video is also informative. Abbey is communicating at a very young age the immediate nature of the digital resources that she wants and reminds us as teachers that we cannot ignore the increasing needs of our students to connect to and interact with digital technologies.

Moving away from primarily print-focused resources, a curriculum that sustains a multimodal perspective can provide the framework for a flexible literacy curriculum that differentiates and values the lives and multiple ways of knowing that learners bring to the classroom (Albers, 2006). An example of this recognition of and valuing is revealed in a study done by Gerber (2009). She found that video games enhanced students' literacy learning when they are allowed to make that connection within the classroom. She explains that video gamers can use their knowledge of game environments to read multiple novels and to expand their interest in writing as well. Some parents and teachers might think that the time spent on video games is not productive, but Gerber's study demonstrates the power of valuing this knowledge to connect these students to literacy activities.

Another consideration is that literacy includes participation as a central component. Literacy enables participation and digital literacies enable new forms of participation (Bruce & Casey, 2012). This participation is described as the literacy of the classroom and not just what the teacher understands about digital technologies nor just what the students' understandings are. Digital technologies can provide the platform for the socially situated experiences that enhance learning.

As we move from page to screen, online reading comprehension (Leu et al., 2008) involves:
- reading online to generate a problem or question from one's social context,
- reading to locate information online,
- reading to critically evaluate information online,
- reading to synthesize information online from multiple sources, and
- reading to communicate and exchange information online with others.

Features

There is a considerable and ever-changing debate about what digital or new literacies are, but a consideration of the elements proposed by Coiro, Knobel, Lankshear, and Leu (2008) provides an effective foundation for understanding our role as teachers regarding digital literacies:

(1) The internet and other forms of information communication technology (ICT) require new social practices, skills, strategies, and dispositions for their effective use;

(2) New literacies are central to full civic, economic, and personal participation in a global community;

(3) New literacies rapidly change as defining technologies change;

(4) New literacies are multiple, multimodal, and multifaceted; thus, they benefit from multiple lenses seeking to understand how to better support our students in a digital age.

Furthermore, traditional methods of implementing best practice for reading, writing, and communication, resulting from a long tradition of book and other print media, are insufficient in the 21st century (International Reading Association, 2009). What differs from earlier models of traditional print comprehension is that online reading comprehension is defined not only around the purpose, task, and context but also by a process of self-directed text construction (Coiro & Dobler, 2007). This construction occurs as readers navigate through a vast informational space to construct their own versions of the online texts they will read. During this process both new and traditional reading comprehension skills are required. The overlap between online and offline reading expands, but also complicates, our understanding of reading comprehension in the 21st century.

Digital literacy includes the personal, technological, and intellectual skills that are necessary to live in a digital world. As the lines between "traditional" and "new" media become imprecise and digital technology becomes increasingly essential for full participation in society, our understanding of digital proficiency has moved from technical ability to include the broader social, ethical, legal, and economic characteristics of digital use (Media Smarts, 2015). This transformative change requires educators to understand the characteristics of digital technologies, stay current to the changing technologies and formats, and seek ways to connect all students to the online reading that is increasingly important for full participation in our society.

Genres

Though genres are important to acknowledge with print texts, this becomes even more critical with websites, because digital texts often rely on hybridity, intertextuality, and social interaction (Chandler-Olcott & Mahar, 2001). Instead of a rigid structure of genres for digital texts, these authors recommend a series of questions to guide students in their understanding. This kind of genre study of websites is more complex and socially situated than traditional print genres. These questions include:

1. How did you find this site? Why did you bookmark it?
2. What else is the site linked to?
3. How is the site used? How else could it be used?

4. How often is the site used?
5. With whom do you interact through and about the site? Do you use or supplement information from it with other media?
6. How is the site organized? What is the relationship between text and graphics? What other sites is it like?
7. What discourse communities might this site represent? Attract? Repel?

Answering questions like these about websites will enable students to consider how they might use, evaluate, and change these digital genres in school and beyond. These questions can be adapted for younger readers.

Content for Instructional Purposes

So how can teachers use digital literacies to access content for instructional purposes? First of all, as teachers we realize that many of our students already access the internet to seek, learn, and transmit information in their everyday lives. It is this behavior that we must connect to the curriculum content in our classrooms. We cannot assume, however, that because our students have digital experiences outside the classroom that they know how to effectively search for information and use digital devices efficiently.

E-readers

One digital device that holds a lot of promise for independent content reading is the e-reader. The use of these digital reading devices with corresponding books has mushroomed in recent years. In fact, in 2011, Amazon.com's sales of digital books surpassed those of print texts for the first time (Bloomberg News, 2011). Features of e-readers can make text more accessible for students who are challenged by reading regular print texts and thus may be a motivational tool. Using an e-reader can allow students to enlarge text, change the font, access definitions, and listen to the text. These interactions with the text actually give the individual some control or self-regulation of the reading process. Studies of young children ages 5–6 using e-readers reveal that their comprehension was increased with the use of "read with dictionary" and "read and play activity" (Korat & Shamir, 2006) as opposed to "read story only." These researchers asserted that the students in this study integrated various pathways to further their understanding of the story.

One child, about 7 years old, in a tutorial program directed by one of the authors was given an e-reader to use. Before the e-reader was introduced, he would not participate in the traditional print activities planned by his tutor and was very disengaged in any type of reading. However, when introduced to the Reading Rainbow (2015) app on an e-reader he became very animated, engaged, and talked about what he was reading to the tutor. He immediately took over the e-reader and quickly maneuvered his way around and began downloading books. Of interest was that he quickly dropped all of the fiction books that were downloaded for trial purposes in the return slot and quickly found the cloud with nonfiction books. He immediately downloaded a book on saber-tooth tigers and began listening to the text as it was read through the e-reader. At times his facial expressions became very enthusiastic as he responded to the information he was hearing and then he would rewind and discuss with the tutor what he had just read. His mother said that while using the e-reader, he showed more interest in reading than ever before. She shared that he did choose to have the books read aloud to him, but at the same time she did catch him reading aloud with it as well.

The results of these interactions with digital texts and devices may make you wonder, what do these e-readers have that traditional texts do not? Middle school students who are challenged by reading were involved in a study using e-readers (Miranda, Johnson, & Rossi-Williams, 2012). These students reported the following benefits to using an e-reader:

- The e-reader has very good books.
- It's cool because it's like a computer.
- I like the dictionary.
- It is easy to use.
- It helps me read faster.
- I like to read more now because the stories are interesting to me.
- I better understand what I read.

These responses may indicate that book selection is easier with an e-reader. One teacher in a study done by Zipke (2013) explained the book selection comments in this manner: struggling readers "hate being in book stores or libraries…it's too much to look at all at once. If they have it in their hands and can search it, it's almost like they have it right in their hands." The comments above may also reveal that the format is appealing, dictionary use is helpful, and comprehension and reading rate may be enhanced with the digital format. These comments may also connect to the motivation to be engaged with reading. More research on using e-readers in elementary schools needs to be conducted to determine if students maintain an interest in using the e-reader and what issues may arise with their use.

With the amount of digital reading websites on the internet, it can be time consuming for a teacher to navigate and choose which websites are the best quality for children's digital reading. Some sites have animation, characters, and story lines that are less than authentic. Investigate websites in the following table to become familiar with those that have quality literature, animation, and reader support.

Online Digital Books Websites

Magic Keys Books	www.magickeys.com/books	Contains digital storybooks for primary and intermediate students. Some stories have accompanying audio.
PlayTales	http://playtales.com/en/	Unlimited books, games, songs, and activities; universal subscription between iOS devices; eight languages to choose from; $4.99 a month or $19.99 annually
Reading Is Fundamental	www.rif.org/kids/readingplanet/bookzone/ read_aloud_stories.htm	Contains fun, animated stories that children can read and sing along to. This site also provides stories read aloud in Spanish.
Reading Rainbow	https://www.readingrainbow.com/classroomeditio/	Unlimited digital books and videos. Students are able to choose their favorite topics (adventure, nature, princesses, etc.) and they each receive a virtual backpack, which they can also customize. Students can also choose to read by themselves or to have the book read to them. App is free and one book is free. More books are available with a subscription for parents for $9.99/month or $49.99/year. Parents and teachers have access to the reading history of each child and the time spent reading. Spanish titles are available. Classroom edition for teachers is in production.
TumbleBooks	http://asp.tumblebooks.com/Default.aspx?ReturnUrl=%2f	TumbleBooks has over 400 audio books of quality children's literature for elementary through high school levels. National Geographic videos are also included. Puzzles and games accompany the books. French and Spanish books are available. Many school and public libraries have a subscription so access and use is free.

Well-designed lesson plans for using e-readers can be found at readwritethink.org. These plans contain a connection to theory, standards, resources, and a step-by-step instructional plan. The standards can be accessed by state with a click of the cursor. The next table highlights some examples of lessons from this website using e-readers.

Sample Lesson Plans with E-readers

Lesson Plans Using E-Readers at Readwritethink.org	
E-book Reading with Response: Innovative Ways to Engage with Text	http://www.readwritethink.org/classroom-resources/lesson-plans/book-reading-response-innovative-30670.html
Going Digital: Enhancing E-book Readers to Enhance the Reading Experience	http://www.readwritethink.org/classroom-resources/lesson-plans/going-digital-using-book-30623.html
Digital Word Detectives: Building Vocabulary with E-book Readers	http://www.readwritethink.org/classroom-resources/lesson-plans/digital-word-detectives-building-30838.html

Inquiry-Based Learning

Digital literacies were once optional, but are now considered as essential for making sense and communicating in our world. Inquiry can be considered as the signature pedagogy for digital literacies as suggested by Bruce and Casey (2012). These researchers propose a framework called the Inquiry Cycle (Shulman, 2005) to guide and support teachers as they move from traditional teaching to the practice of inquiry. This cycle includes the categories of ask, investigate, create, discuss, and reflect, which do not develop in a linear fashion, but with considerable overlap. One of the reasons that inquiry connects well to using digital literacies is that there is a huge difference in answering someone else's questions and formulating your own (Olds, Schwartz, & Willie, 1980).

Thinking about the elementary classroom, let's consider an example of using the inquiry cycle. In one study of the use of digital literacy in Irish primary schools, researchers (Bruce & Casey, 2012) observed a classroom of 23 boys ages 8 and 9 years. The teacher used the framework of the inquiry cycle to guide these students in making an audiovisual slide show on "How to Make a Banana Split." To begin, the teacher led a discussion of needed materials, steps to make a banana split, and key vocabulary. Roles of note taker, photographer, and banana split maker were assigned. The boys then worked in groups taking digital pictures as they made the banana splits. The class then used photo story software to make a slide show of the process. To complete the project, they had to sequence the photos, add text and transition effects to the images, and add background music to the presentation. The boys made four movies which they shared with the whole school.

At first glance, this project looks like a recreation of the traditional "How to" writing assignment often assigned by teachers, but when the layers are peeled back, it is significantly different. Yes, the project work appeared to help the boys develop their print literacy skills through reading, remembering, writing, and following instructions to create the banana splits. There was also a lot of work in describing orally how they made the movies. The class group reflection indicated that they felt they had learned new words and learned how to crop digital images and put them together in a sequence. The use of the digital camera and computer gave the project an added stimulus, and the boys stated that they enjoyed the practical aspects of making the banana split and using technology to capture their work and tell their story. Of course, they also enjoyed eating the banana splits at the end!

On a deeper dimension, these boys learned about the process and practice of inquiry. While the pupils were learning the practice of inquiry, the teacher provided controlled access to inquiry as she directed, modeled, and often scaffolded the inquiry process. She simulated the "ask" stance by arousing and channeling curiosity.

Internet Reciprocal Teaching

Reciprocal teaching strategies have provided effective support for reading comprehension since the original research by Palinscar and Brown (1984). The four strategies—predicting, questioning, clarifying, and summarizing—have proved to also be a strong supportive foundation for teaching students online reading strategies as well (Castek, 2013; Leu et al., 2008). This adaptation is called Internet Reciprocal Teaching (IRT). Using a smart board and an LCD projector, Castek used the reciprocal teaching strategies to teach students how to read a webpage, how to search, synthesize, and evaluate information. An example of one lesson teaches students to read within a search engine. The lesson objectives for reading a webpage included how to query search engines, how to read search results, and how to search within a site to locate specific information. In this manner, students learn how to apply the IRT comprehension strategies and how to search effectively. The end result of this particular IRT lesson is that students can effectively and efficiently navigate the sites that have the information suited to their reading purpose and better understand the content.

Cue cards shown in the following table can scaffold the students in using IRT with online reading.

INTERNET RECIPROCAL TEACHING CUE CARDS (CASTEK, 2013)

Predict	• Explain what kinds of information will be contained on this webpage. • Use cues from the website (illustrations, icons, graphics, or subtitles) to support your prediction. • Identify which hyperlinks will help you navigate through the text to gather information. • Describe the types of information you predict will be hyperlinked.
Clarify	• Look for words, phrases, hyperlinks, or electronic features that are not clear. • Discuss the words, images, animations, or concepts you find confusing or misleading. • Suggested strategies are: examine the context, substitute a synonym, locate the root word, prefix or suffix and use these pieces as supports, ask others, mark the word to look it up later, if it is a hyperlinked word, examine the link to identify supports that may help you (glossary or other online information source).
Question	• Ask questions that begin with who, what, when, where, why, or how. • Ask main idea questions that aid in identifying key ideas. • Ask questions that have under the surface answers. • Ask questions about the navigational path as it relates to constructing a clear summary.
Summarize	• Include the main ideas, not all the details. • Keep the summary concise and focused. • Stick to the point.

Researchers have found that locating and evaluating information is perhaps the central, and most challenging, aspect of developing digital literacy on the internet for students of all ages. Middle school students often revert to older search methods, even when they are not as productive. These results indicate that teachers need to begin instruction in search techniques in earlier elementary years before ineffective search habits develop.

Using a Critical Lens

While digital literacies have the potential to engage students with content and higher level thinking and reading, they also involve some issues. Some problems that teachers are faced with include the availability of technical resources and support, appropriate professional development, time to plan and develop lessons and activities, and useful teaching frameworks.

Additionally, teachers' beliefs and perceptions about the importance and role of digital technologies in school, and their own technological capabilities, are problems that affect teachers' integration of digital literacies in the classroom (Colwell, Hunt-Barron, & Reinking, 2013). It might be important to stop a moment and reflect on your experiences with digital literacies in the classroom. What are your thoughts about including them and teaching students to effectively use them?

As teachers and students engage with digital literacies in their homes and classrooms, there are areas that need careful consideration. One framework that can provide guidance in ethical use of internet resources was developed for Canadian schools. This program is called Use, Understand & Create (Media Smarts, 2015). The Media Smart curriculum contains many components of a digital literacy curriculum and its effective use. Two of the sections that address ethics and security are called (1) Ethics and Empathy, and (2) Privacy and Security. The first, Ethics and Empathy, addresses empathy toward others and making good decisions in digital environments regarding things like cyberbullying and sharing other's content. It is important to note that perpetrators may be more inclined toward bullying online because they do not see or hear the consequences of their behavior, which discourages the development of empathy. Privacy and Security includes managing students' privacy, reputation, and security online; protecting themselves from malware and other software threats; and being aware of their digital footprint, which can be far reaching. Our digital footprints extend further than any text written before and they are instantaneous and often can't be retracted.

What issues have you personally experienced with ethical behavior online? In your opinion what place does examining the ethical use of digital literacies have in our school curriculum?

It is critical that all schools have a framework like the one described above for engaging with the complexities and issues surrounding digital literacies. Such a curriculum is important for reasons beyond content, ethics, and security. Some schools may not make effective use of tools such as e-readers, citing problems with internet use. This issue can be controlled by working with the information technology department on ways to block the internet when using apps for e-books. Instead of decreasing the use of digital literacy tools, teachers could make connections with others in their building or district to decrease roadblocks to their use.

It is also important to note that online literacy has not yet been a component of state and national assessments. Offline literacy has been the assessed reading focus. Often what gets instructional attention is what is tested; teachers need to realize that while we've been slow to add online reading to our assessments, it still needs to be a critical component of our curriculum. We need to realize that we currently have a huge disconnect between what students experience at home with digital literacies and what they find at school. Connecting the digital experiences in both environments would be a strong motivational tool for many students and help them move forward with their literacy development.

Something to Think About!

Digital forms of communication have permeated our society at school, home, and in the workplace. Digital literacies have not replaced traditional print, but the differences between the two formats require teachers to experience and understand ways to use these digital tools to effectively plan instruction for communication, comprehension, and evaluation. Individuals who can efficiently access useful and reliable information and communicate that information effectively will be the most successful in an increasingly global economy that requires high levels of digital literacy.

Technology is just a tool. In terms of getting the kids working together and motivating them, the teacher is most important.
—Bill Gates

Chapter Eight

> *The most important thing that schools can do is not to use technology in the curriculum more, but to use it more effectively.* —John G. Palfrey and Urs Gasser

How important are digital literacies to teaching and learning? According to a Global Work Monitor Survey of 32 countries, employers rated digital skills as 91 on a 1–100 scale (Shine.com, 2014)—a must-have for employees. In order to prepare students for college and the workplace, digital literacy skills must be at the forefront of our teaching curriculum. But it is more than the technology alone and it is more than planning for the future. These digital literacy skills must also be the way our students are engaged in learning and literacy in our classrooms now.

Connecting digital literacies as tools for instruction may seem logical on the one hand, and yet the integration of digital literacies with teaching may prove difficult for beginning and experienced teachers. One framework for understanding this connection is called TPACK (Mishra & Koehler, 2006). This acronym stands for the integration of technology, pedagogy, and content knowledge. Instead of viewing each of these domains in isolation, it is the integration of each area with the others that leads to more dynamic teaching. Figure 8.1 visually demonstrates the TPACK model.

FIGURE 8.1

TPACK Framework
(Mishra & Koehler,
2006)

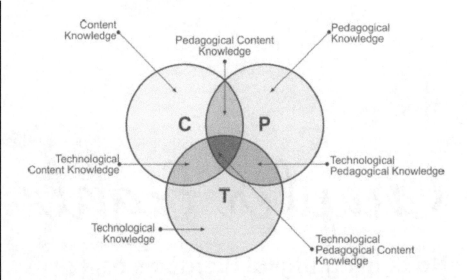

In this chapter, TPACK will be broken down into each major subject area, but first a consideration of learner-centered instruction will provide a theoretical foundation for teaching and learning. A synthesis (Polly & Hannafin, 2010) of the American Psychological Associations' Learner-Centered Principles and research on teacher learning concluded that learner-centered professional development (LCPD) programs should:

- focus on student learning outcomes,
- provide teachers with ownership of their professional development activities,
- promote collaboration,
- address knowledge of both content and pedagogy,
- support reflection on teachers' daily work, and
- include ongoing activities.

These tenets of learner-centered professional development provide a strong framework for implementing the TPACK model of technology, content, and instruction. Teachers can use this framework for their own professional development and transition with it into the teaching and learning of their classrooms.

Now let's take a look at how instruction can be strengthened using the TPACK model in the content areas of social studies, science, mathematics, and language arts. We will use the five literacies as we read, write, speak, think, and listen in the language of content; it is the depth of the five literacies that will empower our teaching and learning.

TPACK in Social Studies

Starting with the content area of social studies and the topic of immigration in the United States, TPACK could consist of online sources about immigration populations, the *Timetoast* timeline website (Todd, 2008), teacher read-alouds, demonstration, use of collaborative groups, and the curriculum standard of why people immigrate from their native countries.

Of course, before starting this TPACK unit on immigration, teachers should use the *Timetoast* program themselves to produce their own timeline, gather resources (both print and online), and plan the sequence of the immigration lessons. As teachers become comfortable with the TPACK model, they can think about it as a way of teaching: they can TPACK their lesson plans to bring technology, teaching, and content together in an effective combination for teaching and learning.

One thing technology can promote is the creation of a product after reading and discussing content texts. This level of learning is higher than literal comprehension because students have to analyze and evaluate what they've read and talked about. Students can represent their learning with videos, diagrams, charts, and graphic texts. While end products to demonstrate learning are not new, the digital resources that are now available in combination with traditional texts can enrich these culminating activities and make them engaging and interesting for students. The integration of content with technology is a natural match with the multitude of online resources available.

Effective integration of technology, pedagogy, and social studies content is seen when technology enables learning that

- is extended beyond that achieved without technology;
- is focused on social studies content and skills and not the technology;
- clarifies relationships among science, technology, and society; and
- enhances the skills, knowledge, and values of good citizenship (Mason et al., 2000).

Frye, Trathen, and Kopperhaver (2010) describe a unit designed for a fourth-grade social studies classroom called Piratical Internet Workshop that highlights the role digital technology can play in enhancing social studies teaching and learning. The focus of the piratical unit was on the National Council for the Social Studies (NCSS, 1994) Thematic Strand II—Time, Continuity and Change, and addressed several social studies themes: (1) the economic impact pirates and privateers had on American colonies; (2) the roles that pirates and privateers played in the wars between England and Spain, the American Revolutionary War, and the War of 1812; (3) the absolute and relative location of major landforms, bodies of water, and ports of call in the early Americas; and (4) the emergence of democratic practices among the pirates.

The unit was organized into two sections. The first section guided students to use Internet resources to "search, read, gather, organize, evaluate, and discuss social studies content" (p. 47). The Internet workshop format developed by Leu (2002) was used as a framework to organize students' activities to enhance learning. Internet workshop (IW) is similar to reading and writing workshop in that students have time to read online independently, make decisions about evaluating what is read, and have the opportunity to share what they learned with others. IW is based on three themes: digital literacies are *deictic*, or regularly change as defining technologies continually change; literacy learning becomes more and more social as multiple literacies emerge from rapidly changing technologies; and learning to learn with changing technologies is at the center of becoming proficient with digital literacies.

These researchers recommend that as teachers begin planning an Internet workshop, they search for Internet sites that provide relevant and useful information written at appropriate levels for students. Once websites are found, then bookmarks should be set. Bookmarking appropriate websites will guide students to critically evaluate the accuracy of information on the Web as they collect, organize, analyze, and share relevant social studies content. Because the Internet sites are bookmarked by the teacher, random surfing is decreased, thereby maintaining safe technology use and efficient use of instructional time.

The second section of this piratical unit provided students with the opportunity to "refine, display, publish, and share social studies content with others" (p. 47). Classroom blogs provided a secure and uncomplicated format for writing, sharing, and validating students' learning. Some examples of students' writing posted in these blogs included poems and digital stories where students took on the perspective of the pirates they researched. Possibilities for collaboration using classroom blogs are endless. Posting opinions and using the blog as a springboard for discussion are two examples.

The authors used this piratical unit to illustrate the importance and possibilities for enriching social studies teaching with the integration of technology. They assert that the research, writing, manipulating, and sharing of information on pirates led to less memorization and deeper understanding of content. Their article, titled *Internet Workshop and Blog Publishing: Meeting Student (and Teacher) Learning Needs to Achieve Best Practice in the Twenty-First-Century Social Studies Classroom*, includes an in-depth description and more information for implementing Internet workshop and blogging effectively, which could be used in any content area. Take a moment to scan this article to help you integrate technology, teaching, and social studies content within the TPACK model.

The following online resources focus on social studies:

DIGITAL SOCIAL STUDIES RESOURCES	
http://sp.uconn.edu/~djleu/titanic.html	An example of a research activity to use during Internet workshop
http://www.ivyjoy.com/rayne/kidssearch.html	A comprehensive list of Internet search engines for kids
http://www.google.com/earth/	Investigating tool of geographic regions via satellites
http://kidsclick.org/	Web search site designed for kids by librarians, with kid-friendly results
https://historytech.wordpress.com/	A social studies curriculum specialist's blog that offers many helpful tips and resources for both social studies and technology
https://www.timetoast.com/	Free online timeline resource
http://www.myhistro.com/	Stories displayed on maps that use text, video, and pictures to create a dynamic timeline mashup
http://www.loc.gov/teachers/	Use of primary sources from the Library of Congress
http://edsitement.neh.gov/	High-quality materials in literature and language arts, foreign languages, art and culture, and history and social studies
http://memory.loc.gov/ammem/index.html	Access to written and spoken words, sound recordings, still and moving images, prints, maps, and sheet music that document the American experience
http://www.nationalgeographic.com	Teaching resources for geography, archaeology and natural science, and the promotion of environmental and historical conservation
http://www.smithsonianeducation.org	Digital access to the vast collections of the Smithsonian; connection to state standards is available

TPACK in Science

Turning to the content area of science as it relates to the TPACK model should begin with the act of inquiry. Scientific inquiry in the classroom revolves around students' active reasoning about scientific phenomena. Until recently, phenomena needed to be staged as physical lab activities or organized in limited ways with relatively static text and graphics. Recently introduced technology tools open up many possibilities of working with phenomena in virtual spaces with a wide range of rich media tools. In addition, these technology platforms provide numerous scaffolds supporting recording and modeling around these phenomena (and underlying concepts) of interest.

Several studies have evaluated teachers' use of digital resources with science concepts, and two key findings have emerged. One suggests that teachers may need help recognizing the cognitive opportunities and limitations of digital tools for the teaching of science concepts (McCormick, Scrimshaw, Li, & Clifford, 2004). This study's results also indicate that teacher support of the students' questioning must be scaffolded deliberately and not left to chance. Another evaluation of a library of digital resources used in Australia and New Zealand asserts that "digital resources have value when they can be embedded in teachers' constructed teaching and learning sequences," not as individual activities simply assigned to students (Freebody & Muspratt, 2007, p. 17). So what do these studies say to teachers, especially beginning teachers who are just starting to build a schema for teaching and learning?

One key component of using digital tools in science classrooms will be the support provided by the school district and/or the state. But what if that support is not readily available? In this case, teachers will have to reach out and educate themselves. Sometimes principals and districts ask what kind of professional development is needed, but if that doesn't happen, teachers can be proactive and locate training and grant resources for using digital tools in science (and other content area) classrooms. The following organizations provide professional development to connect technology to science concepts, and can apply to other subject areas as well.

PROFESSIONAL DEVELOPMENT OPPORTUNITIES FOR DIGITAL TOOLS	
http://edtechteacher.org/summer-workshops/	Organization that provides workshops to support educators in their quest to enrich student learning experiences through emerging technologies
http://www.nsta.org/conferences/	National Science Teachers Association (NSTA), the largest organization in the world committed to promoting excellence and innovation in science teaching and learning
http://mediaeducationlab.com/summer-institute digital-literacy	Innovative Teaching and Learning Workshop with digital media texts, tools, and technologies

In addition to workshops and training to integrate digital applications, Carolyn Fortuna (2015) offers three steps to offset fears of using digital tools and ways to become more proficient in integrating technology with content area knowledge. First, she encourages teachers to find a trusted colleague for assistance in navigating Web applications. There is no shame here! It's possible, Fortuna emphasizes, that you may share some content knowledge with your colleague while learning the steps to a digital application. Second, pilot your new digital tool when the stakes are low and start small. Don't try to change everything at once and do ask for assistance from your digital native students! Finally, take a deep breath, reflect, and revise. Celebrate your success and move forward.

Science and technology are a natural match; and a study by Doyle and Dezuanni (2014) explains some benefits for students who are challenged by traditional print resources in the science classroom. These researchers assert that by facilitating ways of learning science through multimodal means such as filming, photography, editing, and creation of Web-based science profiles, digital media production has the potential to make science more accessible to students. They argue that digital media production can create opportunities for repeated reflection on science content and processes. In traditional science classrooms, they explain, teacher-controlled, explicit teaching practices are often the norm. This kind of teaching can include little control by students in their learning environment. Connecting media arts and engaging multimodal and digital literacies to the science curriculum can encourage experimentation and play and thus permit students to become decision makers in their own learning.

For their study, Doyle and Dezuanni (2014) introduced a digital media production component to a science project with the hypothesis that learning through media arts and the introduction of digital literacies could make science teaching and learning more manageable for fourth-grade students. For this project, which lasted an entire school year, there were four segments, and two dealt with teaching the students how to use digital devices. Part one involved teaching students how to operate laptops, log in, highlight, drag and drop text and images, use software to create text, still images, audio and video files, and use Web design templates. Part two included operating digital still and video cameras to conduct interviews, recording sound, capturing and editing footage. All of the skills for parts one and two were developed in a contextualized manner through a media arts project. Part three included recording a science procedure with a video camera, editing, recording voice over commentary, and adding a title and captions to the video footage. Part four integrated using video cameras and editing software to make a micro-documentary about science topics important to students' lives, using video editing software, voice-over commentary, adding titles and captions, and using music creation software. Notice the time spent on teaching the students how to use the digital devices; this was not a science project that added technology as an afterthought.

This project provides insight into how the use of media arts and engaging multimodal and digital texts can provide practical, accessible, and versatile ways of learning and communicating about science. Furthermore, media arts and science-integrated pedagogies also provide implicit instructional circumstances for science explorations in nonthreatening environments. The researchers view media arts as a feasible pedagogical process for science teaching, which will also enable literacy learning, especially in digital modes. An integrated science/media arts pedagogy has the potential to provide an accessible modality for learning science for all students. This example by Doyle and Dezuanni (2014) provides an effective example of the TPACK model in the curriculum area of science. Notably, it may enhance the participation of those students who experience difficulty communicating and learning science through traditional print modes and increase the opportunities for reflection for all students.

Digital resources offer a variety of cognitive experiences for science learners. Using a combination of text and pictures together can enhance comprehension and retention (Mayer, 2001; Schnotz & Bannert, 2003). Do traditional print resources include text and pictures together? Yes, but online digital resources allow easy access to expansive numbers of texts and pictures so that teachers and students can individually tailor the reading experiences for all students regarding difficulty and interests.

In addition, digital tools can help K-2 students visualize concepts that are difficult to understand, such as the differences between heat and temperature. According to research by Straudt and Forman (2014), digital instruments made the invisible visible and linked these visualizations directly to children's tangible understandings of hot and cold. Using infrared cameras, infrared thermometers, and thermoscopes, the children were able to access and understand the invisible world of thermal energy. Previously, these digital tools cost tens of thousands of dollars, but now are affordable and contain digital screens, permitting interactive examination of temperature and heat concepts in new ways. Rather than using the display of a conventional thermometer with a rising red line, the computer shows a five-inch circle containing moving dots. Probing hotter materials causes the dots to move more quickly and collide more frequently. Working with these digital tools, children began to treat heat not as a hot or cold substance, but as particles that move and bump at different speeds. Students from kindergarten to second grade quickly began to refer to hot as "fast-moving particles" and cold became "slow-moving particles." It is clear that digital tools provided the assistance that these young children needed to make an abstract scientific principle visible and guide them to the understanding of the difference between heat and temperature.

From making science content more accessible for students who struggle with ordinary instructional methods to making abstract scientific concepts visible to allow all students to evaluate and interpret, it is clear that digital tools have many avenues for enhancing science teaching and learning. Stop and think for a moment. Can you see yourself integrating the TPACK model with science content? Consider the different possible content topics to be addressed: friction, volume, matter, magnetism, and condensation are a few examples.

QUESTION TO PONDER

Why do you think it is important for K-2 students to understand that temperature is about fast and slow moving particles?

DIGITAL SCIENCE RESOURCES	
http://classroom-aid.com/educational-resources/science/	A plethora of links to science digital resources—one is the National Digital Science Library
http://siemensscienceday.com/	Digital library of science tools
http://classroom-aid.com/educational-resources/science/	Top free resources for teaching and learning science
http://beyondpenguins.ehe.osu.edu/issue/po-lar-mammals/100-free-web-tools-for-elementa-ry-teachers	100 free Web tools for teachers

TPACK in Mathematics

As stated previously, effective integration of technology occurs when teachers use the TPACK model in their planning and instruction (Mishra & Koehler, 2006; Polly & Brantley-Dias, 2009). Let's keep this idea in mind as we consider technology integration in elementary mathematics classrooms. Pendleton (2013) used various digital tools in an activity called "Problem Solving Mania" where her fifth-grade students engaged in authentic mathematical problem solving in a scenario-based environment. Pendleton asserts that one way to embrace the TPACK model is through the use of video production. Spires, Hervey, Morris, and Stelpflug (2012) emphasized that "video viewing and production are becoming routine practices within our media-rich society" and that "teachers can use video creation as a way to engage students in learning across the curriculum" (p. 483).

BREAKING THE CODE TASKS

Task 1: Encrypt (put in secret code) the practice problem on the website.

Task 2: Write your own secret message in two different codes. Leave your codes behind for the next group to crack.

Task 3: Answer the questions: How did you use math to crack the codes? How did you use reading to crack the codes?

Early finishers: Try to crack the codes that have been left behind.

(Pendleton, 2013)

In Pendleton's classroom, all activities are connected by a common theme. She asserts that choosing the theme is very important because it promotes excitement on the day of implementation. An example of a theme for "Problem Solving Mania" (PSM) is "Action Adventure Movie Heroes." Students are assigned to groups of three and rotate through four stations: computer, planning and design, authentic problem solving, and one that requires physical activity. Two of these stations are described below: computer and authentic problem solving. The role of the teacher during PSM is to assist students in completing their tasks as needed.

BREAKING THE CODE

At the computer center, students were directed to a cryptology website chosen because of its highly interactive nature and wide representation of types of codes. The website also included links to sample codes, information about how to make codes, reasons why codes are used, and interactive capabilities that allow students to type codes and translate them on the computer. Students are then told to read as much information on the website as they need to complete the task. Pendleton explains that she wanted to facilitate an experience in which they were able to read the information they deemed relevant for completing the tasks. Students were given the following tasks.

At the computer center, students used online reading and collaboration skills. For example, students navigated the hypertext and decided which links led to relevant information. In this task, students were expected to be interactive readers who could navigate the design elements of online text (Leu, Kinzer, Coiro, & Cammack, 2004). Given the differences between traditional and digital texts, as noted in chapter 7 of this book, practicing these skills is particularly important for students (Coiro, 2011, p. 358).

Action Problems. At another station, students were given a set of three word problems to solve. Each problem was based on the math curriculum and included details of the theme. The following is a sample problem: "In this movie, there is a scene in which you need to ride a camel. The problem is that you are only 5 feet tall, and the camel is 90 inches tall. How much taller is the camel than you are? If you had a stool that was 24 inches high, would that be tall enough to help you get on the camel? Why or why not?"

Students were expected to collaborate to solve the problems. Once the problems were solved, students were required to write a script bringing the word problem of their choice to life. From an instructional perspective, the acts of drafting the script and making a video of the finished product increased the understanding of the math concepts. Pendleton found that using these multimodal tools during "Problem Solving Mania" promoted the connection of digital literacies, teaching, and math learning more effectively than anything else she had done in ten years of teaching. Wow! What a powerful recommendation!

QUESTIONS TO PONDER

The integration of technology, pedagogy, and math content knowledge as described in Pendleton's classroom occurs more often in summer camps than in regular classrooms. Why do you think this happens? What could be done to change this?

Digital Resources for Math	
http://www.nbcusd.org/PDresources/Math13AmazingDigitalMathresources.pdf	13 Amazing Digital Resources for Math (across grade levels)
http://www.cerias.purdue.edu/education/k-12/teaching_resources/lessons_presentations/cryptology.html	Simple, straightforward cryptology website for kids
http://www.ndlrn.edu.au/using_digital_resources/australian_curriculum_resources/mathematics.html	National Digital Learning Resources Network, an Australian infrastructure for sharing and disseminating digital resources; offers great ideas that also apply in U.S. classrooms
http://www.nsf.gov/news/classroom/mathematics.jsp	Mathematics Classroom Digital Resources sponsored by the National Science Foundation

TPACK in Language Arts

Digital Storytelling. A fifth-grade teacher, Ms. Jenkins, was searching for a way to integrate the teaching strategies that she knew worked well for her students with newly acquired technologies (Shelby-Caffey, Úbéda, & Jenkins, 2014). She was particularly interested in accomplishing this connection of technology and content in ways that would be beneficial to student learning and enhance her teaching. Her school district encouraged teachers to apply for technology grants to integrate content and technology. Jenkins applied for this grant, received it, and used these funds to implement digital storytelling with her students.

Jenkins was also looking for a way to bridge her students' out-of-school literacies with more traditional in-school literacies. Realizing that many of her students used their cellphones outside of school to record videos, she hoped that making movies could serve as a motivational connection between language arts content of script writing and the video tools available on their phones. She wanted her students to be engaged both with technology and with content. Jenkins decided that students' suggestions to make a movie would help to accomplish these goals.

Over a six-week period, Ms. Jenkin's fifth graders participated in a cross-curricular literature focus unit centered around Elisa Carbone's (2007) *Blood on the River: James Town, 1607*. As the text was difficult for some students, Jenkins used a shared reading approach so that all students had access to the text. Literature circles were used for discussion in order to ensure comprehension. Vocabulary lessons targeted concepts important to understanding the text, especially for her ELL students. Mini-lessons included the topics of sequencing, summarizing, creating a script, and editing.

When the novel was completed, students practiced and applied the strategies and skills covered in the mini-lessons. Small groups and pairs of students were each given two scenes from the story. Ms. Jenkins pulled names from a hat and assigned each student one of 24 main events from the novel. Students were asked to illustrate the event, with each illustration contributing to the whole-class discussion about sequencing. The next step was guided practice, in which students worked to retell the story by physically arranging the student-made drawings onto a timeline that was taped to the wall. This activity was followed by a mini-lesson on summarizing, where students chose 10 of the illustrations that would effectively represent the story for someone who had never read it. Once identified, these chosen scenes became the basis for the storyline of their movie. Students used the illustrations from the sequencing lesson as prompts for summarizing the main events of the story. After the completion of the summaries were completed, Ms. Jenkins and her students focused on writing dialogue and stage scenes. They used plays from mentor texts to learn how to create these literary elements. "Wings for the King" (Sroda, 2000) is an example of one of these texts.

The movie began to come together as students worked in pairs to recreate selected scenes. With the summary of a particular scene in hand, students unpacked the details of each scene. Ms. Jenkins provided further scaffolding to students by giving them an advanced story map that prompted them to identify the setting, purpose of their scene, and characters as well as the characters' thoughts, actions, and words. Students reread pertinent sections of the text and used their story map outline as the basis for creating the dialogue for a chosen scene. Bethany used writing conferences to guide her students through the writing process. Groups were responsible for revising, typing, and printing the final version of the script. This process lasted approximately one week.

Students contributed props, staged scenes, and made casting decisions. Critical thinking ensued as these decisions were made. Scenes were between 10 and 35 seconds and were recorded using a flip camera and Ms. Jenkins personal digital camera. The students recorded 11 individual digital stories that were then streamed together to create the movie. iMovie was used to record the voice-over narration. FlipShare software was used to upload the recording from the Flip camera to a MacBook, and iPhoto was used for the still images that were made available for use in iMovie and can be viewed at http://www.schooltube.com/video/5414a077fc418e78db30/Blood%20on%20the%20River .

As Ms. Jenkins reflected on this iMovie digital storytelling project and its impact on teaching and learning, several ideas emerged:

- Her students learned to research, develop a point of view, and create an emotional connection to the content they are learning about. This was a much deeper understanding than surface learning that is easily forgotten. They were also able to collaborate with other students to create a digital representation that reflected their understanding of the content.
- Her students made use of literacy practices in the classroom, which they may have been engaging with outside of the classroom.
- Students who have limited or no access to digital technologies outside of school could expand their learning horizons with these technologies at school.
- Students who may have otherwise been silent during discussion of the text were given a voice through the creation of this digital story.
- Her students applied their expanding knowledge of technology, expressed their creativity, and revealed the contextual lens through which they viewed the story.
- Those writers who struggled benefited from the support of working in a group and worked diligently to make sure that the scripts were accurate for the classmates who would be reading them.
- Struggling readers benefited from hearing Ms. Jenkins read aloud and from the opportunities to practice repeated readings while rehearsing lines.

Ms. Jenkins shared that she was originally hesitant to apply for the district grant and begin this technology project because she considered herself to be a "technophobe." In her own words, after completing the project, she asserted that,

> The only way to become more comfortable with something like digital storytelling and using technology with students is to immerse yourself in the process and learn by doing. Until you actually try it yourself, you have no idea the impact it will have on your students, the motivation it can inspire, the excitement it will create. Knowing what the results will be and what will come of it, I would absolutely do this again. I would jump in with both feet. I've learned

that I'm much more flexible than I thought and that there is nothing I can't do when my students are really motivated. With one project, my students went from passive observers, learning what I told them to learn, to active participants, taking control of their learning. The transformation was incredible and worth every minute I spent on this project. This project turned out better than my wildest imagination. I have repeated this project and others like it and will continue to use technology to transform teaching and learning in my classroom. (pp. 198-199)

Because Ms. Jenkins was willing to be proactive, as described earlier in this chapter, and made decisions to improve her own professional development with technology, she was able to experience the power and opportunities of integrating digital literacies in her language arts classroom. Imagine what could happen when you take charge of your own professional development regarding the integration of technology, instruction, and content. The possibilities are endless!

QUESTION TO PONDER
What could you do to take advantage of professional development for including technology in your content area?

Blended Literature Circles. Another example of implementing TPACK in language arts curriculum is a study explained by Bromley and colleagues (2014). These graduate students implemented literature circles in a blended arrangement with some of the assignments done in an online layout and some in a face-to-face design. What these researchers learned included several key points for teachers:

- Obtain permission for internet access. In addition, teachers should check their schools' policy on blocked sites and request a waiver if necessary for assignments like this one.
- Provide appropriate classroom technology. Students need access to computers and the internet.
- Provide instruction in navigation skills (e.g., keyboarding, spelling, scrolling, scanning, cutting, pasting).
- Provide instruction in critical digital literacy. Children need instruction in how to determine the currency, accuracy, and authenticity of a website.
- Use digital assignments to differentiate instruction. Matching children to roles that may suit them best by connecting with an interest or strength can be beneficial.

Text Sets. The information about text sets found in chapter 3 can be easily and effectively used with digital texts or a combination of digital and traditional print resources. These texts of various genres, media, and levels of difficulty provide depth and allow teachers to differentiate instruction for interest and reading ability. Students can be guided toward assembling their own text sets on topics of interest. An example of a digital text set for intermediate students on the topic of cyberbullying follows:

DIGITAL TEXT SET RESOURCES FOR CYBERBULLYING (THE READING AND WRITING PROJECT, 2015)	
http://stopcyberbullying.org/teens/are_you_a_cyberbully.html	Are You a Cyberbully? Rating Scale
http://www.stopcyberbullying.org/why_do_kids_cyberbully_each_other.html	Why kids cyberbully each other and how to prevent it
http://www.stopcyberbullying.org/why_do_kids_cyberbully_each_other.html	"Because I can" – When kids act out violent fantasies online

QUESTIONS TO PONDER
How do you see technology integrated into the instruction in your field experience classrooms? What ideas can you use and what ideas do you have that might enhance this use of technology and content?

DIGITAL RESOURCES FOR LANGUAGE ARTS	
www.edudemic.com/8-steps-to-great-digital-storytelling	8 Steps to Great Digital Storytelling
http://digitalstorytelling.coe.uh.edu/	Educational uses for digital storytelling
https://www.ischool.utexas.edu/technology/tutorials/graphics/imovie/1create.html	How to create an iMovie project
www.voki.com	Representing a character through speech
www.toondoo.com	Cartoon creation website; also available as an app
www.moovly.com	Easily created animated videos and other multimedia content
http://sourceforge.net/projects/audacity/	Audacity: free software used for recording and editing sound

Something to Think About!

Admittedly, for many teachers, and especially for beginning teachers, integrating technology, teaching, and content curriculum within the TPACK model can be overwhelming to say the least. There are several reasons, however, why this consideration is not only important, but essential. First of all, the format can prevent using technology for technology's sake. When the focus is solely on the technology, we can end up in effect with what might be called a "computer worksheet"—a fill-in-the-blank model of one right answer. Integrating digital resources with teaching and content, on the other hand, can increase the opportunities students have to analyze, evaluate, and create during the learning process. Another reason to include the TPACK model in lesson planning is the amount of digital resources available and accessible, which also assists in differentiating instruction. Capitalizing in deliberate ways on the digital resources and knowledge students bring into the classroom can also be motivating and promote engagement with learning. Although integrating technology, instruction, and content knowledge is not an easy undertaking, investigation and preparation using the TPACK model can provide a strong foundation with exceptional learning for teachers and students.

"It is important that teachers integrate technology into their classroom curriculum for the educational benefits technology may bring to learning, instead of just integrating it for the sake of using technology."

—*Matheson, Wilson, and Wright (2014)*

SECTION V
Making Research Real

$E=MC^2$

$\pi = 3.14159265$

$V_f = V_i + at$

$a^2 + b^2 = c^2$

H_2O

?

X

5cm

90

$M = 5.9736 \times 1024\ kg$

2, 3, 5, 7, 11, 13, 17, 19, 23, 29, 31, 37, 41, 43, 47, 53, 59, 61, 67, 71, 73, 79, 83, 89, 97

Chapter Nine

The Inquiry Process: Exploring and Evaluating

"Every effort must be made in childhood to teach the young to use their own minds." —Eleanor Roosevelt

Now that you have knowledge of strategies to support student learning of the language of content through the five literacies and many tools for designing effective instruction, let's look at the inquiry process. This provides students an opportunity to practice all of the strategies and skills that have been presented thus far in previous chapters. Now you will see how students apply numerous strategies and skills to explore and evaluate, seeking answers to questions and often generating more questions in the process. Through inquiry, students use complimentary processes of assimilating and accommodating new information to construct new knowledge.

Assimilation is taking in new information, to use and build on existing schema.

Accommodation is when new information does not fit with existing schema and new knowledge must be developed or existing schema changed to adjust for the new information (Piaget & Cook, 1952).

Much like the phrase, "I can see your wheels turning", the graphic below reflects thinking and the inquiry process. The mind is intertwining cognitive processes and information as questions are generated, answers are sought after, conclusions are established, and additional questions are created.

Children and Inquiry

Curiosity and an innate impulse to learn are fundamental human attributes. Think of an inquisitive child asking endless questions. Often the child begins with "*why*" and then asks questions sometimes so rapidly that it is difficult to respond to one before the next comes.

Inquiry is a natural process that can provide children personal experiences and direct feedback that they need to construct knowledge and shape their views of the world. Think about a child who jumps in a puddle and sees the water splash. The child does this over and over and then realizes that the water in the puddle is no longer splashing. The child stomps, but no more water can be displaced, and so moves to another puddle and starts over again. What has this child learned through personal inquiry and actions? Inquiry begins very concretely, as in this example; however, as children get older their inquiries become less concrete and require higher levels of thinking and means of accessing information in other ways.

So how can teachers model and teach inquiry to make a difference in the way children acquire information and understand scientific concepts? Too often, children's inquiry is squelched when they enter school and they are only afforded opportunities to hear content information from the teacher and read preselected materials with no attention given to interest and multimodal learning experiences. Teaching and encouraging children to think for themselves, to think critically and reason, to construct knowledge and to work with others is a goal we must strive to reach. As educators we must provide opportunities for students to become information literate and develop informational fluency.

When children engage in inquiry, it provides them with endless learning experiences, but also provides teachers a window to "see what and how" students are thinking, what they know, and the direction they may need to access new information. However, before you can begin teaching and guiding students through the inquiry process, it is important to understand what it is and why it is important. It is also important to keep in mind the outcome we strive for as educators—for students to become fluent in informational literacy.

DO SCHOOLS KILL CREATIVITY?

During a TED Talk, Sir Ken Robinson did an excellent job of posing the question teachers should be asking…. How can I keep the creativity alive in my classroom?! Watch his talk and then think about how you will keep it alive in your class!

https://www.youtube.com/watch?v=iG9CE55wbtY

Inquiry-based Learning

Inquiry-based learning is a student-directed process and can be linked to John Dewey's philosophy that education begins with the curiosity of the learner, and Jerome Bruner's theory of discovery learning as noted in previous chapters. Inquiry-based learning is an approach to learning whereby students locate sources of information to increase their understanding of a problem, topic, or issue. It espouses investigation, exploration, research, and study (Kuhlthau, Maniotes, & Caspari, 2007). It is inspired by a constructivist approach to teaching and learning, which theorizes that there are many ways of constructing knowledge and that teaching the skills of "how to learn" is more important than finding information; learning the process is essential. At the heart of inquiry-based learning is asking questions—but not just any questions. These must be questions that students really care about and have a desire to seek information for answers.

Through inquiry-based learning educators help students to identify and refine their inquiry by developing real questions, then guiding them through the research and reporting processes. An inquiry-based learning approach is flexible and encourages a collaborative learning environment. Additionally, the inquiry can include the entire class working on a single question, small groups working on the same or different questions, or students working independently. However, it is important that all students in the group truly care about the question at hand.

The inquiry-based approach can work with any age group. As presented at the beginning of the chapter, children are naturally inquisitive, but as you work with students to encourage the spirit of inquiry, keep in mind the importance of developmentally appropriate practices and activities for younger children. Then, when working with older students, you can encourage and engage them in much more sophisticated questioning and research processes.

Inquiry-based Learning versus Traditional Approaches

According to research, active learning is a powerful tool. Through engagement and active learning students develop abilities that are crucial for learners, such as critical thinking, problem solving, teamwork, and becoming critical consumers of informational literacy. Children's inquiry provides them opportunities to receive accurate feedback based on the outcomes of their self-directed inquiry. The inquiry process encourages learners to be self-directed and provides motivation for learning, which is important as students seek information and build knowledge. Often the instructional approach in content areas is explicit teaching, where the teacher selects the content and covers the material. According to Harvey and Daniels (2009) there are substantial differences between the inquiry approach and the traditional coverage approach to learning. An advantage of the inquiry-based approach acknowledges that children, especially those from lower socioeconomic status, have what researcher Luis Moll calls "funds of knowledge" that are often ignored by traditional approaches to teaching. Teachers can make their classrooms more inclusive and culturally responsive through awareness of the knowledge children acquire from their family and cultural backgrounds (Moll, Amanti, Neff, & Gonzalez, 1992). The inquiry-based learning process validates the personal experiences and knowledge that all children bring to the learning process.

So how is inquiry-based learning different from traditional approaches to teaching? In the traditional teaching approach, teachers are the source of knowledge and the ones who determine what information is important. There are differences in how each teacher shares the information and teaches, but the topics are selected and projects are driven and assessed by the teacher. In contrast, with inquiry-based learning students ask questions which selects topics, projects are driven by students, and both teacher and students take part in the evaluation and assessment process. Students are inspired by being in the driver's seat of their own learning, thus becoming motivated by ownership through their role in decision making. Keeping this in mind, though, don't get the wrong idea in thinking inquiry-based learning is unstructured; the process is structured differently. In fact, for the teacher there is more planning, preparation, and responsiveness needed—just as the structure is different, so is the role of the teacher.

So let's look at a comparison of these two approaches. As you read through the differences think about what this might look like in the classroom. Which approach do you see as most beneficial for student learning, and why?

Inquiry Approach	versus	Coverage Approach
Students have choice and voice		Teacher directs and selects
Collaborative work among students		Students work independently
Questions created and content explored		Factual information is provided
Strategic and critical thinking		Memorization of facts
Authentic exploration and investigation		Incidental learning
Self-directed and student responsibility		Compliance and completion
Teacher is facilitator and models inquiry		Teacher is expert
Student is creator of knowledge		Student is receiver of information
Interactive and discussion driven		Sit and get method
Multiple resources are explored		Textbook or single text dependent
Multimodal learning experiences		Listening to information presented
Engaging in cross-disciplinary connections		Single subject studies
Intrinsic motivation—purpose		Extrinsic motivation
Audience and sharing of information		Short-term learning and moving on
Authentic and self-assessment		End of unit paper-based test

Adapted from: Harvey, S., & Daniels, H. (2009). *Comprehension and collaboration.* Portsmouth, NH: Heinemann.

As you can see from the comparison above, inquiry-based learning is a powerful student-centered approach to teaching and learning. The process engages students in knowledge construction through **hands-on/minds-on** learning opportunities. It is important to understand that inquiry-based teaching and learning is not an instructional approach or a teaching method, but a process where teachers and students are engaged learners, seeking answers to real-world questions. It should not be considered as having students research and complete a project. Through inquiry, students gain deeper understandings as they research and seek information and determine what information is needed to answer real and relevant questions; and as they do this, they develop information literacy.

How does inquiry help develop information literacy? The term "information literacy" refers to the set of skills required to locate information sources, access the information, then be able to evaluate it and use it efficiently, effectively, as well as ethically. In an information-rich society, where we have access to vast amounts of information, our critical evaluation is central to social, economic, and personal well-being. In essence, information literacy skills are as essential as basic reading and writing. It is imperative that students achieve a level of information literacy that will allow them to find, assess, and use information to succeed in school, the workplace, and their personal lives. Information literary includes a set of abilities that allow an individual to identify information when it is needed and apply those abilities to locate, evaluate, and effectively use the required information.

Information Literacy and Fluency

Fluency is generally associated with the ability to read text accurately, quickly, and expressively; as well as to speak and write to express oneself easily and articulately. Additionally, the levels of fluency change according to purpose in communication, audiences, and experiences (Callison, 2004). However, information fluency should be considered in much broader context as the ability to effectively apply strategies required to move confidently among a wide array of resources to effectively and efficiently find answers. Let's look more closely at the mindfulness an information literate possesses, along with the skills and abilities needed for information fluency as noted in the following chart.

An Information Literate Person:	Skills and Abilities Needed for Information Fluency:
Knows the importance in determining what information is needed for a specific purpose	Ability to transfer information acquired from multiple sources for a specific purpose
Understands the importance of effectively accessing information from multiple sources	Employ skills to use technologies and a variety of other methods to locate and present information
Knows why we must critically evaluate sources and information	Ability to express ideas effectively and in a variety of ways
Understands how to efficiently note only the information needed	Can work collaboratively and communicate effectively with others
Understands that new information increases knowledge and builds schema	Ability to identify and use multiple skills and strategies to find and select needed information
Understands how the information fits into a greater context	Ability to think critically and creatively to solve problems based on derived evidence
Understands ethics in accessing and using information for individual purposes or goals	Intertwines the five literacies throughout the entire process

Inquiry Process

Developing strategic information literacy skills takes practice. Students need many opportunities to navigate through the inquiry process. There are steps that must be followed for inquiry to be effective and these steps must be modeled and students guided to become more proficient at inquiry. Figure 9.1 depicts the five steps of the inquiry process and essential questions that should be considered within each step. As educators, we must keep in mind that while students are gaining factual information, answering questions, and problem solving, it is equally important for students to be able to name and explain the strategies they are using and why they are using them, as they become fluent in the language of content.

What does inquiry look like in the classroom? What does it look like outside of the classroom? What is the teacher doing? What are students doing? What are the steps in the process? How do teachers effectively guide students through inquiry? Most teachers have many questions about how to effectively guide students through the inquiry process, especially when you have a classroom of students and only one of you. So let's look closely at what should take place within each of the steps. When beginning inquiry, there must be much modeling and guiding, but students will become expert inquirers if they have many opportunities to experience the process.

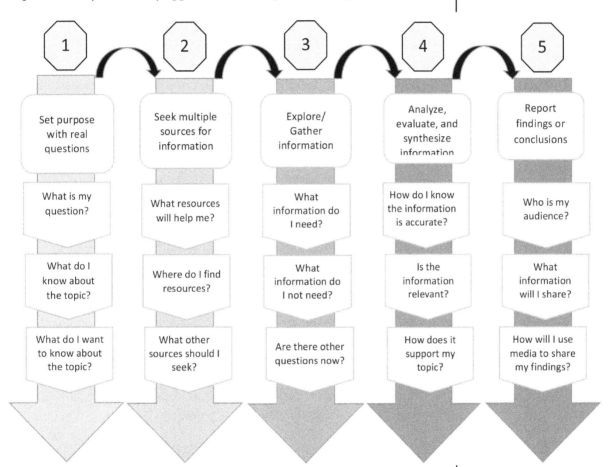

FIGURE 9.1 Steps and Considerations in the Inquiry Process
Adapted from: Education Development Center. (2012). YouthLearn Initiative.

The Art of Questioning

The foundation of inquiry-based learning is helping children ask real and relevant questions; therefore, in order to do so, teachers must develop the art of questioning. As the facilitator in the inquiry process, teachers must model the essence of inquiry. Most topics can be explored through an inquiry-based approach; however, the question must be worded in a way to guide the process for deeper understanding. Depending on how a question is posed, it can provide an open door for discussion or it can close the door completely. For example, consider the responses you may get from students based on how you ask one of the following questions: "Most of you don't know anything about marine mammals, do you?" versus "Do any of you know about marine mammals?" versus "What do we know about marine mammals?" The first question is negatively worded and assumes the students know nothing about the topic, although the second question is a bit more positive, it is a closed question evoking only a yes or no response. The third question, on the other hand, invites student input by validating and activating prior knowledge. The discussion will provide a starting point for inquiry. Our goal is to help students develop a question that will guide them to find what they really want to know. To do so effectively, teachers must be aware of some characteristics of good inquiry questions. It is also important to practice both questioning and listening skills to determine what questions encourage inquiry and what topics students truly care about researching, to drive them to seek answers to their burning questions. Consider the following when helping students develop and refine questions:

- *The question posed must not be answered by locating a simple fact.* When did the first man walk on the moon? This can be a quick search to find the date and the answer. Now think about this question: What factors and considerations led to the success of the *Apollo 11* mission and Neil Armstrong becoming the first man to walk on the moon? This question cannot be answered in quick or simple terms, but will require students to search resources, compare, analyze, synthesize, interpret, and draw conclusions.
- *The question should not be so direct that students will not be encouraged to explore.* Consider the question, What is rap music? Students may have some ideas as to what rap music sounds like or is, but the question does not stimulate inquiry. Develop the question further: What musical and historical influences contributed to the creation of the rap music genre? This question can be researched with depth and will provide a context for broader understanding of the development of rap music.
- *Students must be able to answer the question or draw conclusions through research.* Why did dinosaurs become extinct? This would be a difficult question to answer as it remains a mystery. It is believed that the last of the dinosaurs died around 65 million years ago. Scientists rely on fossils and other evidence to develop theories to determine potential causes for the demise of dinosaurs. Therefore, a more answerable question would be: What evidence has led scientists to develop theories and support beliefs as to why dinosaurs died out long ago?
- *The question must not be personal or subjective; it must be objective to provide a basis for an answer.* Which book by Chris Van Allsburg, Ju-

manji (1981) or *Polar Express* (1985), provides the reader the most exciting and unpredictable journey? This is subjective and personal to the reader and true inquiry is not needed to answer the question. However, consider: What was the inspiration for Chris Van Allsburg's writing and illustrating award-winning children's books? This can be explored and an objective and informative response to the question can be presented, as there are primary and secondary sources available to answer the question.

Now let's look deeper at the inquiry process. How do we begin the inquiry process with students? We must guide students through the process of selecting a topic, posing a strong inquiry question, and planning an inquiry. It is helpful for students to see the big picture—what the process is going to look like. The following chart provides a guide for students to develop an overall plan and organize for inquiry. However, before students work on their I-Plan it would be best to use the chart to first model, then as guided practice so students understand the purpose of the plan and how to create one that will be effective throughout their inquiry. It is also important to note that the plan can change and be adapted, but it provides an opportunity to record the student(s) vision for the inquiry and see the overall process. A good way to start inquiry is to have students jot down their thinking on an I-Plan. Take a look at what needs to be considered in developing an inquiry plan. (See Appendix for a blank I-Plan template for individual students and a template for group inquiry.)

INQUIRY PLAN (MY I-PLAN)

Topic: a broad subject from which several subtopics may emerge

Subtopics: more narrow topics generated from the overarching topic

Potential Inquiry Question: students generate a question that can be refined

Possible Sources to Explore: includes a wide array of materials; you may refer to page 48 for a list of accessible texts to explore

Audience: classmates/teacher/parents/other classrooms/display/upload to a website, etc.

Presentation Format: oral/digital/documentary/written format from mentor text/ speech/research paper/photo essay/poster/model/roleplay historical character, etc.

Evaluation: self-evaluation by student/peer/teacher/outside individual

Other Considerations:

Timeline: when inquiry will begin and the goal for completion

STEP 1: SETTING PURPOSE FOR INQUIRY BY DEVELOPING REAL QUESTIONS

Students determine their topic of inquiry and then begin the process of developing their overarching question and possibly sub-questions that relate to the topic and may help answer the "big" question. Brainstorming is a good way to begin. Having students stop and jot topics of interest, why they are interested in the subject, and questions they may have about the topic can help them begin their inquiry process. Students must understand that they are seeking answers to their own questions, not looking for someone else's answers or conclusions. It is also helpful for students to participate in discussions to expand ideas and extend thinking. Then, when they begin to select and narrow the focus of their topic, questions begin to percolate. Students think about what they know and what they want to know, which helps them generate and refine their question and the inquiry. In step 2, when students begin searching and gathering information, they may find that their inquiry question changes or needs further refinement. The inquiry process ebbs and flows as students move through steps. (See appendix for copy of chart.)

Step 1: Posing and Refining My Question(s)	
Inquiry Question or I-Question:	
Sub-questions:	
What I know about the topic	What I want to know about the topic

BECOMING FLUENT IN THE LANGUAGE OF CONTENT

The Heat is on! HOT Questions (Higher Order Thinking). For most educators, Bloom's taxonomy is a concept woven through the numerous efforts put forth to create critical learning environments. We strive to be conscientious of our own questions posed to students so they become aware of the questions they pose for themselves. Essentially, Bloom and his colleagues advanced how teachers taught as well as set the expectations for determining the level of student learning through the 21st century. Since 1956, teachers have designed lessons that incorporate the six learning objectives: recalling *knowledge*, the *application* of knowledge, *analysis* or breaking down of knowledge, *synthesis* or putting together knowledge, and the *evaluation* or judging of knowledge (Forehand, 2011). While the hierarchy of learning can still play true today, the higher order thinking skills of the mid-20th century can seem a bit one dimensional for millennial teachers and students in our classrooms today. Not to worry! Bloom's colleagues also saw a need to bring new dimension to the taxonomy of learning. In 2001, they came together to evolve the learner objectives to reflect the dynamic types of learning happening in and out of the classroom. *A Taxonomy for Teaching, Learning, and Assessment* (Anderson & Krathwohl, 2001) quite simply moved the HOT (Higher Order Thinking) skills into the 21st century by changing the key terms from nouns to action-based words. Using verbs allows teachers to bring in the cognitive process to the learning environment. Let's take a look.

> **Millennials**—referring to those born between 1985 and early 2000s.

1956 HOT Skills	2001 HOT Skills	New HOT terms mean:
Evaluate	Creating	Putting elements together to form a coherent or functional whole; reorganizing elements into a **new** pattern or structure through **generating**, planning, or producing.
Synthesis	Evaluating	**Making judgments** based on criteria and standards through checking and critiquing.
Analysis	Analyzing	Breaking material **into parts**, determining how the parts **relate** to one another and to an overall structure or purpose through differentiating, organizing, and attributing.
Application	Applying	**Carrying out** or using a procedure through executing, or implementing.
Comprehension	Understanding	**Constructing meaning** from oral, written, and graphic messages through interpreting, exemplifying, classifying, summarizing, inferring, comparing, and explaining.
Knowledge	Remembering	Retrieving, recognizing, and recalling relevant knowledge from **long-term memory**.
Notice the change in the importance of "creating/synthesis." It has moved to the highest level. (Chart modified from Anderson & Krathwohl, 2001, pp. 67-68.)		

I am sure you noticed that the new HOT skills add depth to the thinking process with phrases like "long-term memory," "constructing meaning," "relationships," and "generating new." Even the Knowledge/Remembering skill requires the authentic use of knowledge to become part of the language the student uses highlighted by the need to recall relevant knowledge from long-term memory. In other words, students need to become fluent speakers and users of that knowledge to make it long term.

Anderson and Krathwohl (2001) offer two additional dimensions in the revised Bloom's taxonomy. The first dimension is the Cognitive Process Dimension (the verb terms just discussed), and the second is the Knowledge Dimension. In the revised version, the Knowledge level includes Factual Knowledge, Conceptual Knowledge, Procedural Knowledge, and Meta-Cognitive Knowledge. These four dimensions actually bring a deeper and more powerful presence to the lower level HOT skill of Knowledge. Too often we "looked down" on this skill as lesser surface level knowledge, but now when paired with the six Cognitive Process Dimension skills there is meaningfulness to the "knowing" of knowledge at each HOT skill. Before, we took Synthesizing as being the ultimate HOT skill. Now, when we ask students to be "Remembering Knowledge," there are four layers of remembering to be worked through! If we want students to remember content knowledge so they can become fluent users of that knowledge, we want them to move beyond just thinking or recalling lists of facts, but also to explain and become aware of appropriate uses for that knowledge. Take some time to visit the Oregon State University website. Their interactive revised Bloom's chart offers more detail regarding each verb listed in the following table.

> **Ah-Ha!**
>
> Now you know where that term **metacognition** came from!

Knowledge Dimension	Cognitive Process Dimension					
	Remembering	Understanding	Applying	Analyzing	Evaluating	Creating
Factual Knowledge	List	Summarize	Classify	Order	Rank	Combine
Conceptual Knowledge	Describe	Interpret	Experiment	Explain	Assess	Plan
Procedural Knowledge	Tabulate	Predict	Calculate	Differentiate	Conclude	Compose
Meta-Cognitive Knowledge	Appropriate use	Execute	Construct	Achieve	Action	Actualize

Chart adapted from the Oregon State Bloom's Taxonomy table. (2005). Designer Dianna Fisher http://oregonstate.edu/instruct/coursedev/models/id/taxonomy/#table

Playing with HOT Questions! So you are probably thinking right now… how do I get my students to ask the HOT questions? While students are naturally curious, they sometimes need our help to become aware of the types of questions that really dig deep into their inquiry. So the answer is quite simple…they need to play with crafting HOT questions so they begin to understand what it really means to unlock the door to their interests and inquiry pursuits. Let's look at the chart, "Playing with Hot Questions." This chart takes common Bloom's Knowledge skills and creates a matrix for depth and breadth in relation to question formation. Notice the arrows. Question terms that are put together starting at the top left are simple and relate to "remembering" or listing of facts. These types of questions will provide some information but with little depth. For example, "who is…" will only generate a simple response about the topic. With that said, questions like these are valuable in the big picture of conducting inquiry as they usually can be uncovered fairly easy and offer quick reward for the inquiry process. To really uncover more, the learner needs to dig deeper by moving to the right of the matrix, which leads to forming question such as "why should…" or "Why might… ." Again, let's look at the chart, particularly the shaded boxes. Questions that use stem starters along the shaded diagonal form a very HOT set of questions and guide inquiry from the simple to the complex pursuit of knowledge! As inquiring minds, we want to have a sampling of these types of questions in our inquiry plan. With this matrix as a starting place, students are able to play with forming questions and develop awareness that inquiry should be based on a range of simple to complex questions.

Complex →

Simple ↓

Playing with HOT Questions						
	Is/Isn't	Did/Didn't	Can/ Can't	Will/Won't	Might/ Might Not	Should/n't Would/n't Could/n't
Who	▓					
What		▓				
When			▓			
Where				▓		
Why					▓	
How						▓

Cubing and crafting questions. Question cubes can be bought online or made (see the appendix for a black line master for cubing questions— children's building blocks such as those in the picture can be used as well!) and are designed to use Bloom's thinking skills to interact with crafting HOT questions. Each of these cubes has a set of question term stems. One cube has the terms found going down the left of the matrix, while the other cube has the terms going across the top. The cubes make it concrete for learners to play with questions to determine if the question will take them far enough down the path of inquiry. By simply rolling the cubes, students play with forming the start of inquiry questions. The more they interchange these terms to form question, the more fluent they become at speaking the language of a researcher.

Playing with HOT Questions—Titanic						
	Is/ Isn't	Did/ Didn't	Can/ Can't	Will/ Won't	Might/ Might Not	Should/n't Would/n't Could/n't
Who					X	
What	X				X	
When						
Where					X	X
Why		X				
How						

WORD #1	WORD #2	BODY OF QUESTIONS—Titanic
What	might	What might it have been like to be a first class passenger on the *Titanic*?
Where	would	Where would someone board the *Titanic*?
Where	might	Where might the shipwreck be located?
What	is	What is the *Titanic*?
Who	might	Who might have worked behind the scenes to run the *Titanic*?
Why	did	Why did the *Titanic* sink?
Example of using the question cube to craft HOT questions with the topic of the *Titanic*.		

BECOMING FLUENT IN THE LANGUAGE OF CONTENT

As with most learning experiences, the guided inquiry learning you provide will be crucial for students to form the ability to transfer the art of building questions to their everyday inquiry purposes, both formal and informal. You might start with discussing and selecting a whole class topic of interest. Once a topic is selected and a purpose for exploring made, begin "playing with HOT questions" to narrow down what specifically the class would like to discover. You can guide this process with the reference sheet found in the appendix called "Playing with HOT Questions." Role the cubes and check off where it falls on the matrix. Is this a simple or complex question? Why? Write the two terms into the chart. This is an excellent opportunity to conduct a Think Aloud to demonstrate what a researcher "thinks" when forming questions as well as to show that somctimes a thinker has to play around with the way a question sounds before it sounds just right. Keep rolling and involve the students in determining how to form the questions as well as what level of question it is. Will the question touch the surface of what they want to uncover? Or will it help them dig deeper into the topic? Critical question forming takes time, so practice often playing with HOT questions to get the hang of it. Very focused and diverse types of questions are the first steps toward having a positive experience with inquiry. So what do we do now with these questions? Organizing inquiry and selecting sources becomes the next skill needed to navigate the inquiry process and for learners to become critical consumers of new knowledge.

> What would this "think aloud" sound like? Try to imagine how you would let learners in on your own thinking process!

STEP 2: ORGANIZE INQUIRY AND SEEK MULTIPLE SOURCES FOR INFORMATION

Organizing for Inquiry—The Research Folder. While asking questions and creating a focus for inquiry is definitely important, knowing what to do with these questions *and* how to organize inquiry is equally necessary. Too often learners set off to explore a topic but lack navigational skills to explore all the information they are about to uncover. Learners can get lost in the sea of facts and not know how to approach it or where to begin. When this happens, learners might resort to an all-or-nothing mode of gathering information, meaning they will record everything they find or omit sources all together. That is where the Research Folder comes in handy. This is a clean and organized way for students to stay focused on the direction of inquiry. Let's get this started with setting it up!

Setting up the Research Folder

Materials: manila folder, 12–3x5 index cards, markers, 1 envelope

Step 1
- Take three index cards and three different colored markers.
- Turn the index card upside down and color in the margin space a different color for each card.
- Number each card #1, #2, #3

(More questions can of course be used)

Step 2
- Take card #3 and tape down in the middle/center of the folder. Follow with the other cards layering so that the color strip shows.

Step 3
- Write 'Data' on the envelope. Push the flap in and tape down on all four sides. This will be discussed later in the chapter.

Step4
- With the remaining nine index cards, separate into three cards for each question.
- In the top open margin, color a large dot the same as question #1.
- Repeat for each set of three cards matching to question #.
- Store these in the Data envelope so the colored dot can easily be seen.

As learners set off on their inquiry journey seeking the answers to their questions, they need to stay focused on finding sources that will lead them down the path to answering these questions. It becomes necessary for the main questions to stay in the forefront of their inquiry. They act like a road map

BECOMING FLUENT IN THE LANGUAGE OF CONTENT

for learners. With so much information to explore, how will they know if a source is relevant or deep enough to meet their needs? Simply, it will be the questions. Sources should be cross-referenced with the questions to make sure they keep to the focus of the journey. Sure, there may be some side trips along the way that learners were not expecting to uncover. If the source is that intriguing, then learners can file that as "Extra Interesting Info" in the Research Folder as it might be useful later. This can be stored in a manila envelope attached to the back of the Research Folder. These might later be used as "Interesting Facts to Know" in a section of the finding.

Let's return back to the *Titanic* questions from the Playing with HOT Questions activity. There were more than three questions formed in the example, so now the learner will need to narrow down to those that will matter most. These will be the main questions used to gather information. For the Research Folder, each one of these questions will be written on a taped down card for easy reference throughout the inquiry.

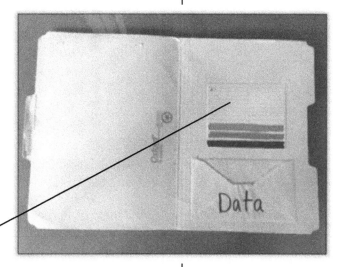

Titanic Example:

- Orange card #1—Who might have worked behind the scenes to run the *Titanic*?
- Purple card #2—What might it have been like to be a first-class passenger on the *Titanic*?
- Green card #3—Where might the shipwreck be located?

With questions selected and organized, it is now time for the inquiry journey to begin. From books, magazines, online resources, personal interviews, and even movies… the sea of information is about to be sailed!

Seek multiple sources of information. Research can be a daunting task, even for the most experienced researchers. Thus, **teaching** the research process can be an even bigger challenge. Assuming a systematic role in modeling the process and organizing research is essential. The search must be planned and students need to learn how to record their searches so they may refer back to them if needed. It is also essential that students learn to evaluate sources as they select materials for their inquiry. We want them to find accurate information from reliable sources. Students must be guided through the process of evaluating a variety of sources. Providing many opportunities to practice seeking and evaluating sources will develop their adeptness for looking through a critical lens as consumers of information. When beginning a research or inquiry one may think they will not be able to find enough information about a topic; more often the opposite is the case. However, finding many resources is one

TIP: Don't forget to refer learners to the chart in Chapter 4, "More on the Depths of Informational Text." Learners should be familiar with layers of informational text. These will mostly correspond with the type of question they asked. If the question was more on the simple side of the question matrix, a concepts book will do the trick. If the question was more complex, they will be more prepared to seek out a survey or specialized book, saving them time in the process!

thing, but most important is finding really **good** information that is relevant to the inquiry. So let's look at some resources and ways to locate information and determine credibility and reliability of the materials.

Primary and secondary sources are important considerations when conducting research. This was introduced in Chapter 6 with Discovery Learning Circles, but let's look at these more closely through the lens of a researcher. Primary sources are firsthand accounts of an event or materials such as a letter, diary or journal entry, map, speech, painting, photograph, autobiography, personal interview, or other forms of original work. Whereas, secondary sources are secondhand accounts of primary sources or materials in which primary sources have been analyzed and interpreted by others, such as movies and book reviews, translations, pictures, graphics, or authors using quotes from primary sources. The benefits of using primary sources is the firsthand account of the events. This provides the most reliable information and a perspective that can only come from original works.

Searching the Internet. Often individuals begin research with the World Wide Web, while this may be a source, there are also many other accessible texts that may provide excellent and more reliable information about the research topic. The Web can be a good place to start, but should not be relied on as the only source. At times, online searches can be frustrating and time consuming—taking the researcher down many trails that do not connect with the inquiry topic. Additionally, references or sources on the Web are not always investigated to determine credibility of the source. Is should also be noted that GOOGLE is a search engine and a good place to get ideas; however, it is not a website or a source that can be cited in the research. Lastly, while Wikipedia may be tempting, it is not always reliable as a source and should be viewed as a means to find additional, more credible sources at the end of each section or subject.

Considerations in Evaluating Websites. The best way to determine if a website is reliable is to look closely at the URLs (there is a three-letter clue in the address). Think of this as "decoding" the URL, or Internet address. The origination of the site can provide hints to the site's mission or purpose, and its reliability of information. You will likely recognize the most common domains:

- .edu—educational organization or higher education institution
- .com—commercial or business site
- .org—an advocacy website or nonprofit organization
- .gov—federal government
- .mil—military
- .net—network organization or Internet provider

Knowing something about the domains as a search is conducted is the first step. Below are some questions that can help in evaluating web pages as reliable sources. Most library web pages provide a detailed listing of ways to evaluate web sources. Researchers should look at the criteria from multiple lenses before making a decision regarding the quality of a source. Here are some things to consider.

Locating a site:

- How did you find the page?
- Was it found via a search engine or through library databases?
- Was the site recommended by someone or noted in a text as a resource?

Authority of source:

- Is there an authority noted on the page?
- Is the author's name clearly visible?
- Are the credentials of the author noted and relevant to the information?
- Is the author affiliated with the organization or institution?
- Is there contact information included for the author or website contacts?

Accuracy of information:

- Is the information presented objectively and accurately?
- Are sources and facts cited?
- Is there a bibliography?

Web page:

- Is there advertising on the page? If so, what is the relationship between the content and the advertisement?
- Is the page current and the links functional?
- When was the web page created and last updated?

STEP 3: EXPLORING SOURCES AND GATHERING INFORMATION

As students locate and gather information they should begin recording and organizing the data for later analyzing and synthesizing of what is truly needed. Here are some guiding questions that can help students as they take notes:

- Is the information directly related to my inquiry and question(s)?
- Is the author and/or the organization or institution reliable and knowledgeable?
- Is the information needed historical or more current?
- How accessible is the information?
- Is there bias or is the information presented in a neutral way?
- Is there enough information to support your inquiry or is it just surface level?

This is a great process to model through a think-aloud with two or three sources on a topic and discuss how you as a researcher can determine the value of a source or lack thereof in seeking answers. The chart that follows can help students record and organize their sources when determining what information is available. (A copy of the chart can be located in the appendix.)

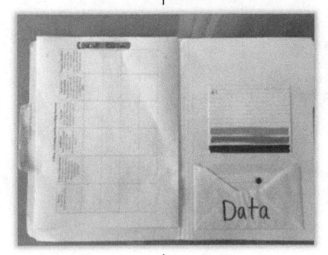

Matching Information in the Research Folder. Let's return to the Research Folder. The I-Plan chart can be stored on the left side of the folder. By using a two-hole puncher and a metal brad, additional charts can be added as needed. While recording the useful sources of information, a technique for organizing the information that specifically answers the initial research questions is to return to the color codes. If learners have decided the resource is relevant to be added to the chart, they should also cross-reference it to the specific questions. On the chart, the last column records the question number or color dot that matches the question. By using the organization tool, students can easily match factual information back to the question when it is time to report findings.

The next step will be for students to take a much closer look at each of the sources they have selected to evaluate and decide what is relevant and reliable and what is not.

I-Plan: Locating and Recording Sources

Source	Author Information	Audience	Current	Important Information	Inquiry Question
Record URL or text/material citation	Is the author an expert or just sharing opinion? What information about the author's credentials is available?	Who is the intended audience of the information—educational or point of view?	Is the website or text up to date? When was the information posted, updated, or written?	What information is in the source that will help with my inquiry? Record page numbers or quick reference links.	Which inquiry question does this most closely answer? Add the question # or a color dot that matches the research question.

Step 4: Analyze, Evaluate, and Synthesize Information

By this point in the inquiry process students have gathered a number of sources for information. They have sorted through many different materials, done some weeding out, and have already learned a considerable amount about their topic and inquiry. Now, it's time for students to select the most relevant information and finalize the focus of the inquiry. Through the process, focus can shift a bit as new information is located or new questions evolve, which may change the path of exploration. This is the beauty of learning through inquiry as it is a continual ebb and flow of searching and evaluating, narrowing and broadening focus to capture the answers one seeks. The following chart provides a good way for students to evaluate sources to determine those that will best suit their inquiry needs. (A copy of the chart can be located in the appendix.)

Notetaking—Summarizing and Paraphrasing. After students select the materials, it is time to summarize information through notetaking. Learning to take notes effectively is a skill that will benefit students throughout their lives, but it takes lots of practice. Summarizing and paraphrasing both mean restating information in your own words; however, summarizing should reduce the information represented in the source by at least 50%, whereas paraphrasing will be lengthier. Students often have difficulty determining what the most important information is, thus they resort to paraphrasing the entire section or selection of information.

A good way for students to practice summarizing it to use a strategy such as SQ3R (survey, question, read, recite, review). Students are provide a section of text to look over, develop questions about what they will be reading, read the text, restate what they read, then review the text. The next step is to have students select key ideas from the text and then write a summary in their own words—making sure to reduce the length by at least half of the original work. Graphic organizers are a great way to record key ideas and noteworthy information.

Lastly, as student record information be sure to teach them how to include direct quotes. At times the words of a primary source can be a significant piece in the inquiry. A powerful quote can add to the relevancy of the research and often contributes just the right "punch" needed to support the inquiry project.

I-Plan: Analyzing, Evaluating, and Synthesizing Information

Source Record URL or text/ material citation	Relevance Rate 1–3 1: not much relevance 2: somewhat relevant 3: extremely relevant	Reliability Rate 1–3 1: not much reliability 2: somewhat reliable 3: extremely reliable	Current or Dated Note the date of information	Accessibility of Information East to navigate and locate information?	Bias or Objective	Use or Lose the Source Yes or No

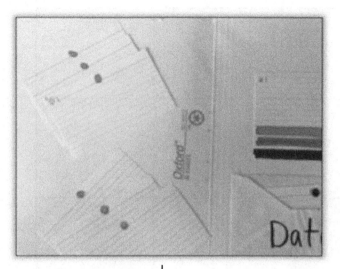

Organizing Information in the Research Folder. A part of the Research Folder we have not addressed yet are those extra index cards from the material list in the Data envelope. For every question, a learner will want at least three supporting facts found during the inquiry process (of course there can be more!). As students are recording page numbers and quick reference links in the I-Plan chart column "Important Information," they can also begin organizing the collected quotes and summarized or paraphrased facts related to their main questions. When the Research Folder was created at the start of the inquiry process, we pre-made color-dot notetaking cards that already corresponded to a research question. The learner can begin with these cards to match information back to the questions as they travel down the inquiry path. This is a time-saving organization step! The color-dots make it easy to notice if certain questions are being overly researched, or if others are not being addressed. If there are too many of the same colored-dot data cards or too few, this is the time to reflect on why. Is the learner spending too much time on a question? Is the question too deep or random? Does the researcher need to find new sources that can provide more information to that question? Does the question need to be tossed? The data cards help learners stay focused on the main questions and give each question equal attention. They will be a great organizational tool as they come to the next step of reporting finding or conclusions.

STEP 5: REPORTING FINDINGS OR CONCLUSIONS AND WORKING FROM THE RESEARCH FOLDER

At this point, students have their data and are ready to think about ways to share their findings. This is a good time for students to use a quick checklist.

MY INQUIRY OR I-CHECKLIST

o Have I gathered enough information to answer my question(s)?
o Do I have all of my sources and references?
o Have I analyzed my data closely to be sure it is connected to my inquiry?
o I have used graphic organizers, sticky notes, note cards, some other system, to help me sort and organize my data?
o How do I want to present the final product?
o What will I need to create the product?
o How will I share my work?

Working from the Research Folder. Once the learner has determined that the questions have been explored deep enough (a nice rule of thumb for a beginning inquirer is three to six fact/data cards per question), the color system can once again assist with data organization. Going back to the Research Folder, the student now can remove the three main questions guiding the inquiry AND bring together the corresponding fact color-dot cards into one group. The cards can be evaluated once again for repetition or usefulness. Together with the question card, the cards can be arranged and rearranged in an outline format to prepare for reporting the findings either formally or informally. This

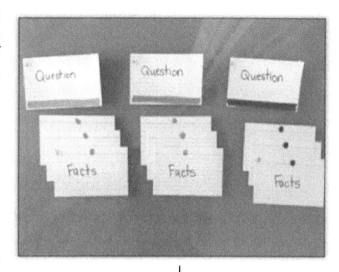

provides a visual organization of how the data all fits together. Whether the findings from the inquiry will be in written form or visual, the learner has a concrete layout to move forward.

Now students must decide on creating a final product to share with the intended audience. They are ready to transform all of the factual data they have collected and synthesized into a product of their own creation. It is likely that they have been thinking and planning for the final format, but this is where planning is really important. Students should think about key ideas in their research and organize their notes to determine a good introduction, the main points to cover, and the conclusion to sum up their findings. They may record information on sticky notes or index cards, which will allow them to physically move them around and manipulate their data and organize thoughts. Being able to visualize the big picture and where the smaller pieces fit can help immensely. It also provides a basis to see where there are gaps that need attention.

Graphic organizers are also a great tool for students to use in sorting and categorizing information. Based on the format of the final product, students should use different types of organizers. For example, a concept map could be helpful if they are creating a photo essay, a sequence chart when developing a digital slide show, or an outline when developing a script for a newscast. The graphic organizer must be carefully selected to best help students visually take in the information and see how it flows in creating the final presentation.

Reporting Formats. Students must now decide on a format. Here are few ideas they may consider:

Pamphlet	Poster	Chart
Brochure	Report	Research paper
Editorial	Letter	Journal entries
Newscast	Reporter on the scene	Panel discussion
Debate	Speech	Video
Song or lyrics	Script for movie or play	Digital presentation
Web page	Map	Painting
Collage	Create a model	Speak from character's perspective
ABC book	Demonstrate an experiment	Mural

Whatever students choose to do to present their findings is their choice; however, they should keep in mind their strengths and interests, as well as the format that would truly showcase their inquiry project. The final product is the method of effectively communicating the information students have gathered and analyzed to answer their inquiry question(s).

Sharing most often includes an oral presentation which can be nerve-racking for many individuals. It is not easy to get up in front of peers and speak, but there are a few things that can teach students to help them remain focused and interesting.

- Don't include every detail that you recorded—summarize your findings and share the most important ideas or conclusions you discovered through your inquiry.
- Try to maintain eye contact with the audience and look at everyone, not just one or two people.
- Don't fidget with things.
- Speak clearly and loud enough for everyone to hear.
- Make sure the audience can see what you are presenting—position yourself in a central place.

Let's look at the end product of an inquiry of a fourth-grade student, Blayne. He was interested in learning more about the Battle at the Alamo. So through his search he began to formulate questions:

- Why was there a battle at the Alamo?
- Who was involved in the battle?
- What did the Alamo look like?
- Who were the leaders of the battle?

After researching, Blayne noted his information in charts and selected the information necessary to answer his questions. When determining how to share his findings he decided to write a report to summarize information to answer his questions. Then he wanted to show his classmates the layout of the Alamo and note the significant locations within the walls. Lastly, as he presented his findings he decided to tell about the battle from William B. Travis' perspective as the commander of the Alamo. He used his model to present events that took place and summed up his presentation with Travis' very own words, which he quoted in his report, "I shall never surrender or retreat…Victory or Death."

Blayne chose to use several modes of sharing his findings because it was a topic he was truly interested in and wanted to explore. The more he learned, the more he wanted to do with his findings to really tell the story of this historical event. By including many dimensions to his inquiry process and final project, he developed a deeper understanding through finding the answers to his inquiry questions noted above.

THE ALAMO
By, Blayne (4th grade)

When Mexico declared independence from Spain a new life had begun. Three years later, in 1824, the nation was divided into 24 states. Because not enough people lived in Texas it was not a state, this made native born Texans feel left out. They supported colonization. Because increasing the population was the only way to become its own state. In 1830 Mexico tried to stop settlement in Texas. This made Texans VERY ANGRY! The Texas revolution from 1835-1836 changed it all.

The Battle of the Alamo is the one we will never forget! February 23, 1836 the Mexican Army arrived at the Alamo where the Texans were sheltered. The very next day William B. Travis, commander of the Alamo, sent a letter to Sam Houston asking for help. The letter was published in a newspaper and considered as one of the most desperate pleas for help ever sent. William B. Travis wrote "I shall never surrender or retreat…Victory or Death".

On March 6, 1836, as many as 250 Texans held out for 13days then fell in the battle that only lasted 90 minutes. Among those lost were James Bowie a famous knife fighter and Davie Crockett a famous frontiersman, both from Tennessee. Only a few women and children survived the Alamo battle.

There is much debate about the siege at the Alamo, but it will always will be remembered for its heroic fight against all odds, where men made the ultimate sacrifice for freedom. These men sacrificed their lives, but it allowed General Sam Houston enough time to put together an army who were able to defeat General Santa Anna's Mexican army in the next battle at San Jacinto, April 21, 1836, which only lasted 18 minutes, to give Texas its freedom.

This is Blayne's model of the Alamo. After completing his research he decided to create a model of the Alamo using some photos he discovered through his inquiry process. He numbered significant locations on the Alamo and added a legend at the top for the audience.

Evaluating and Reflecting

At the end of an inquiry it is important to encourage students to evaluate and reflect on **what** they learned through the process **how** they learned. Whether students worked independently, with a partner, or a group, there should be a self-evaluation for students to grow as reflective thinkers. It is important for students to think about their learning, level of commitment to the inquiry and to the group, contributions to the project and group, and the effectiveness of their role in the process. The following self-assessment provides students with some guiding questions to assess their own learning process as well as group participation.

My Inquiry Self-Assessment	
Inquiry Topic:	Content: What are the key things I learned through my inquiry? ▪ ▪ ▪
What I learned through the process:	
Steps in the inquiry process	
Working with a group	
How I like to learn	
How well did my final product reflect what I learned?	
What would I do differently?	

Self-Assessment of Group Participation	
I contributed to the group by:	
What went well in the group?	
What did not go well?	
What should the group do next time to fix the issue?	
How can I make the group more effective?	

Final evaluation should include criteria to assess the inquiry process. A rubric is one of the best methods of assessing the overall learning as it occurred. Here is a sample rubric that can be modified based on the level of the student and the final product expectations (see resources section for a copy).

Assessment of Inquiry Process			
Inquiry Process	Proficient	Moving toward Proficient	Developing
I-Planning — Selecting a topic, setting purpose with real questions, narrowing focus, determining current knowledge and learning goals	Demonstrates critical thinking and independence in topic selection and questions	Moderate assistance is needed to narrow focus of topic and developing questions	Much guidance is needed to develop inquiry focus and questions
Searching — Seeking multiple sources for information, maintaining focus on topic; selecting relevant sources, locating a variety of texts	Searches and locates a variety of sources with little assistance, selects relevant sources	Needs assistance in locating sources, minimal variety of sources are selected	Much guidance is needed to search for and select sources, has difficulty selecting relevant materials
Processing — Establishing focus of inquiry by recording relevant information, making connections and inferences, refining inquiry	Demonstrates understanding of focusing on relevant information, refines inquiry	Needs some guidance in recording relevant information and refining inquiry	Needs much guidance to determine and record relevant information
Organizing — Analyzing, evaluating, synthesizing information, organizing and planning for final product and sharing	Demonstrates ability to organize information and determine format for final product	Needs minimal assistance in organizing information and determining final format	Need much guidance to organize and plan for final product
Sharing — Communicating findings or conclusions effectively based on audience, sharing new understandings of topic	Clearly and effectively communicates understanding of inquiry	Communicates findings but has some difficulty with clearly stating findings	Has difficulty communicating findings and explain product
Final Product — Clear focus on topic, information reflects new understanding and demonstrates progression of learning through the process	Demonstrates evidence of new understanding and meaningful inquiry process	Demonstrates understanding of inquiry but needs some expansion in presentation	Does not reflect understanding of the inquiry process and product; lacks in content and presentation

Something to Think About!

When students have completed their inquiry they may feel as though they reached the finish line of their journey. However, inquiry is not a linear process, it is cyclical. The process involves thinking about new information and then rethinking as students reach new levels of knowledge, connecting and building on what they already know. As students navigate through the inquiry process they likely develop new questions—which is a good thing. A really good inquiry should encourage more inquiry. Both students and teachers should reflect, asking questions such as *What have I learned? What more do I want to learn? What might I do differently next time? Where do we go from here?* Inquiry provides students rich learning opportunities to explore their interests and a purpose for learning. Most importantly, the five literacies are interwoven in the inquiry process to increase fluency in the language of content.

"Learning is not attained by chance; it must be sought for with ardor and attended to with diligence"— Abigail Adams, 1780

SECTION VI
Instructional Resources
Appendix

$E = MC^2$

$\pi = 3.14159265$

$V_f = V_i + at$

$a^2 + b^2 = c^2$

H_2O

$M = 5.9736 \times 10^{24}$ kg

2, 3, 5, 7, 11, 13, 17, 19, 23, 29, 31, 37, 41, 43, 47, 53, 59, 61, 67, 71, 73, 79, 83, 89, 97

Content Language Checklist

5 Literacies		Reading
		Writing
		Speaking
		Thinking
		Listening
Learning Skill		Vocabulary
		Content Comprehension
		Content Organization
		Content Ownership
Type of Strategy		Front Loading
		Back Loading
		Whole Lesson
Appropriate Level		Lower Elementary (PK-1)
		Upper Elementary (2-6)

Learning about Informational Text

Semantic Feature Analysis Chart

Things about Informational Text

Types	Organization	Access Features
Concept	Enumerative	Headings/subheadings
Photographic	Sequential	Sidebars
Survey	Chronological	Bulleted information
Reference	Question/answer	Insets
Specialized	Narrative	Easy to Navigate?
Other	Other	

Patricia Durham, 2011

TEXT FEATURE ANALYSIS CHART

Title of Text:

Author:

Analysis of features	Included?	What would you suggest to make the text better for the reader?
Is the copyright date of the book recent so the information is current?	Y or N	
Is there information about authors to help readers know their background and experience about the topic of the text to determine credibility of information? Are they qualified to write about the subject?	Y or N	
Does the table of contents provide an efficient way for readers to find information?	Y or N	
Are chapter titles included that will guide readers to specific categories of information?	Y or N	
Do chapters or sections have headings and subheadings to direct readers to specific topics?	Y or N	
Is there an index to guide readers to specific pages containing information they may be seeking?	Y or N	
Is there a glossary to help readers find definitions for specific vocabulary? Does it include a pronunciation guide to help readers learn how to say the words?	Y or N	
Is some information accentuated for readers by the use of different fonts, italicizing, bolded print, underlining, or bullets?	Y or N	
Are the graphics visually appealing and support understanding of the content?	Y or N	
Do the visual images have captions and explanations to support understanding of the graphic and the subject matter?	Y or N	
Is the information presented in parts or chunks so the content can be understood?	Y or N	
Does the style the author used to present the content make the topic and the text interesting and engaging?	Y or N	

CAUSE AND EFFECT

Signal words: _____

Signal questions: _____

| Cause | • Effect:
• Effect:
• Effect: |

| Cause | • Effect:
• Effect:
• Effect: |

| Cause | • Effect:
• Effect:
• Effect: |

CAUSE AND EFFECT

Signal words: _____

Signal questions: _____

Cause	Effect

Cause

Effect

Cause

Effect

Summarize what you have learned.

SEQUENCE OR PROCESS

Signal words: _____

Signal questions: _____

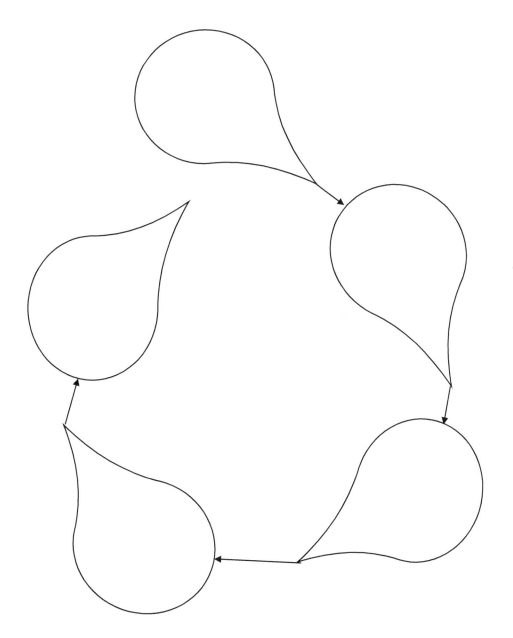

What was the step-by-step process and what was the outcome?

SEQUENCE

Signal words: _____

Signal questions: _____

Significance

Event 2

Significance

Event 3

Significance

What are your conclusions and interpretations?

BECOMING FLUENT IN THE LANGUAGE OF CONTENT

COMPARE AND CONTRAST

Signal words: _____

Signal questions: _____

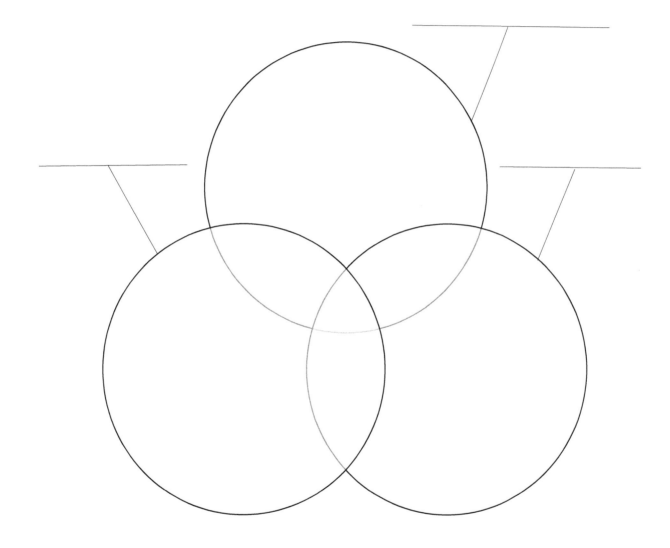

COMPARE AND CONTRAST

Signal words: _____

Signal questions: _____

How are they similar?

How are they different?

Be Specific

What are you conclusions?

What are your interpretations?

Content Discovery Learning Circle Self-Assessment/Group-Assessment and Reflection		Yes	No	Somewhat/ how to improve
Preparation	I completed all the required reading by the agreed on time.			
	My materials were prepared and detailed.			
My Role and responsibility	I completed my role and presented ideas clearly.			
	I used textual evidence to support my thinking.			
	I stayed on topic and was thorough in finding and presenting information.			
As a group member	I gave others the opportunity to participate and did not talk over others.			
	I listened thoughtfully as others shared their thoughts and information.			
Working together as a group	We worked together to make sure everyone participated.			
	We used respectful communication skills, only one person talked at a time.			
	We made sure each person provided evidence from the text.			
	We stayed focused and actively listened to each other and collaborated as we discussed the content.			
	All members were involved in the discussion and we encouraged each other to share.			

Group Assessment Reflection:

What was the most successful part of the discovery learning circle process?

What was the best thing about how your group worked together?

What was one problem that occurred in the group? How did the group solve the problem?

What should your group do next time to improve the discovery learning circle process?

What did you learn from the entire discovery learning circle process?

Step 1: Posing and Refining My Question(s)
Inquiry Question or I-Question:
Sub-questions:

What I know about the topic	What I want to know about the topic

PLAYING WITH HOT QUESTIONS!

Question types: Check the box that represents the word combination selected when the cubes were rolled. Then complete the following chart to craft questions. Questions should fall along the shaded diagonal line.

Complex →

	Remembering		Understand			
	Is/Isn't	Did/Didn't	Can/Can't	Will/Won't	Might/Might Not	Should/n't Would/n't Could/n't
Who						
What						
When						
Where						
Why						
How						

Complete the chart below as you roll the cubes and generate new questions about your inquiry. Then form the remaining part of the question to match your inquiry topic.

WORD #1	WORD #2	BODY OF QUESTION

I-Plan -- Locating and Recording Sources

Source	Author Information	Audience	Current	Important Information	Inquiry Question
Record URL or text/ material citation	Is the author an expert or just sharing opinion? What information about the author's credentials is available?	Who is the intended audience of the information—educational or point of view?	Is the website or text up-to-date? When was the information posted, updated, or written?	What information is in the source that will help with my inquiry? Record page numbers or quick reference links.	Which inquiry question does this most closely answer? Add the question # or a color dot that matches the research question.

I-Plan: Analyzing, Evaluating, and Synthesizing Information

| Source
Record URL or text/ material citation | Relevance
Rate 1-3
1-not much relevance
2-somewhat relevant
3-extremely relevant | Reliability
Rate 1-3
1-not much reliability
2-somewhat reliable
3-extremely reliable | Current or Dated
Note the date of information | Accessibility of Information
East to navigate and locate information? | Bias or Objective | Use or Lose the source
Yes or No |
|---|---|---|---|---|---|---|
| | | | | | | |
| | | | | | | |
| | | | | | | |

MY INQUIRY OR I-CHECKLIST

o   Have I gathered enough information to answer my question(s)?

o   Do I have all of my sources and references?

o   Have I analyzed my data closely to be sure it is connected to my inquiry?

o   I have used graphic organizers, sticky notes, note cards, some other system, to help me sort and organize my data?

o   How do I want to present the final product?

o   What will I need to create the product?

o   How will I share my work?

MY INQUIRY SELF-ASSESSMENT	

Inquiry Topic:	Content: What are the key things I learned through my inquiry?
	
	   ▪
	
	   ▪

What I learned through the process:	
Steps in the inquiry process	
Working with a group	
How I like to learn	
How well did my final product reflect what I learned	
What would I do differently	

SELF-ASSESSMENT OF GROUP PARTICIPATION	
I contributed to the group by:	
What went well in the group:	
What did not go well:	
What should the group do next time to fix the issue:	
How can I make the group more effective:	

BECOMING FLUENT IN THE LANGUAGE OF CONTENT

Assessment of Inquiry Process			
Inquiry Process	Proficient	Moving toward Proficient	Developing
I-Planning Selecting a topic, setting purpose with real questions, narrowing focus, determining current knowledge and learning goals	Demonstrates critical thinking and independence in topic selection and questions	Moderate assistance is needed to narrow focus of topic and developing questions	Much guidance is needed to develop inquiry focus and questions
Searching Seeking multiple sources for information, maintains focus on topic; selects relevant sources, a variety of texts are located	Searches and locates a variety of sources with little assistance, selects relevant sources	Needs assistance in locating sources, minimal variety of sources are selected	Much guidance is needed to search for and select sources, has difficulty selecting relevant materials
Processing Establishing focus of inquiry by recording relevant information, makes connections and inferences, refines inquiry	Demonstrates understanding of focusing on relevant information, refines inquiry	Needs some guidance in recording relevant information and refining inquiry	Needs much guidance to determine and record relevant information
Organizing Analyzing, evaluating, synthesizing information, organizing and planning for final product and sharing	Demonstrates ability to organize information and determine format for final product	Needs minimal assistance in organizing information and determining final format	Need much guidance to organize and plan for final product
Sharing Communicating findings or conclusions effectively based on audience, shares new understandings of topic,	Clearly and effectively communicates understanding of inquiry	Communicates findings but has some difficulty with clearly stating findings	Has difficulty communicating findings and explain product
Final Product Clear focus on topic, information reflects new understanding and demonstrates progression of learning through the process	Demonstrates evidence of new understanding and meaningful inquiry process	Demonstrates understanding of inquiry but needs some expansion in presentation	Does not reflect understanding of the inquiry process and product lacks in content and presentation

References

Afflerbach, P. (2004). Assessing adolescent reading. In T.L. Jetton & J.A. Dole (Eds.), *Adolescent literacy research and practice* (pp. 369–390). New York: Guilford.

Albers, P. (2006). Imagining the possibilities in multimodal curriculum design. *English Education, 38*(2), 75–101.

Allan, K., & Miller, M. (2005). *Literacy and learning in the content areas: Strategies for middle and secondary school teachers.* Boston, MA: Houghton Mifflin.

Anderson, L.W., & Krathwolh, D.R. (Eds.). (2001). *A taxonomy for learning, teaching and assessing: A revision of Bloom's taxonomy of educational objectives: Complete edition.* New York: Longman.

Anderson, R.C., & Pearson, P.D. (1984). A schema-theoretic view of basic processes in reading comprehension. In P.D. Pearson (Ed.), *Handbook of reading research* (pp. 255–291). New York: Longman.

Ardac, D., & Akaygun, S. (2004). Effectiveness of multimedia-based instruction that emphasizes molecular representations on students' understanding of chemical change. *Journal of Research in Science and Teaching, 41*(4), 317–337.

Ausubel, D.P. (1960). The use of advance organizers in learning and retention of meaningful material. *Journal of Educational Psychology, 51,* 267–272. doi:10.1037/h0046669

Ball, D.L., & Feiman-Nemser, S. (1988). Using texbooks and teachers' guides: A dilemma for beginning teachers and teacher educators. *Curriculum Inquiry, 18*(4), 401–423.

Barron, R. (1969). The use of vocabulary as an advance organizer. In H.L. Herber & P.L. Sanders (Eds.), *Research in reading in content areas: First year report* (pp. 29–39). Syracuse, NY: Syracuse University, Reading and Language Arts Center.

Beck, I.L., McKeown, M.G., & Kucan, L. (2013). *Bringing words to life: Robust vocabulary instruction* (2nd ed.). New York: Guilford.

Bloom, B.W., & Krathwohl, D.R. (1965). *Taxonomy of educational objectives: The classification of educational goals, by a committee of college and university examiners. Handbook 1: Cognitive domain.* New York: Longman.

Bloomberg News. (2011). Amazon.com says Kindle e-book sales surpass printed books for first time. Accessed April 10, 2015 from www.bloomberg.com/news/2011-05-19/amazon-comsays-kindle-electronic-book-sales-surpass-printed-format.html

Brabham, E.G., & Villaume, S.K. (2001). Building walls of words. *The Reading Teacher, 54*(7), 700–702.

Bromley, K., Faughnan, M., Ham, S., Miller, M., Armstrong, T., Crandall, C., & Marrone, N. (2014). Literature circles go digital. *Reading Teacher, 68*(3), 229–236. doi:10.1002/trtr.1312

Brookhart, S. (2010). *How to assess higher-order thinking skills in your classroom.* Alexandria, VA: Association for Supervision & Curriculum Development.

Brozo, W. (1990). Learning how at-risk readers learn best. *Journal of Reading, 33,* 522–527.

Bruce, B., & Casey, L. (2012). The practice of inquiry: A pedagogical 'sweet spot' for digital literacy? *Computers In The Schools, 29*(1/2), 191–206.

Buehl, D. (2006). Think Alouds: The A-B-C's of coding text. Retrieved from http://wilearns.state.wi.us/apps/Print.asp?ap=&cid=610

Callison, D. (2004, Spring). Information fluency. School Library Media Activities Monthly.

Castek, J. (2013). Supporting online reading comprehension through Internet reciprocal teaching. *California Reader, 47*(1), 38–43.

Chall, J.S., Jacobs, V.A., & Baldwin, L.E. (1990). *The reading crisis: Why poor children fall behind.* Cambridge, MA: Harvard University Press.

Chandler-Olcott, K., & Mahar, D. (2001). Considering genre in the digital literacy classroom. *Electronic Literacy in School and Home: A Look into the Future, 5*(4). Retrieved from http://www.readingonline.org/electronic/chandler/

Christ, T., & Wang, X.C. (2010). Bridging the vocabulary gap: What the research tells us about vocabulary instruction in early childhood. *Research in Review. Young Children, 65*(4), 84–91. www.naeyc.org/files/yc/file/201007/ChristWangOnline

Clay, M. (1991). *Becoming literate: The construction of inner control.* Auckland, NZ: Heinemann.

Coiro, J. (2011). Predicting reading comprehension on the Internet: Contributions of offline reading skills, online reading skills, and prior knowledge. *Journal of Literacy Research, 43,* 352–392. doi:10.1177/1086296X11421979

Coiro, J., & Dobler, E. (2007). Exploring the online comprehension strategies used by sixth-grade skilled readers to search for and locate information on the Internet. *Reading Research Quarterly, 42*, 214–257.

Coiro, J., Knobel, M., Lankshear, C., & Leu, D.J. (2008). Central issues in new literacies and new literacies research. In J. Coiro, M. Knobel, C. Lankshear, & D.J. Leu (Eds.), *Handbook of research in new literacies* (pp. 1–21). Mahwah, NJ: Erlbaum.

Colwell, J., Hunt-Barron, S., & Reinking, D. (2013). Obstacles to developing digital literacy on the internet in middle school science instruction. *Journal of Literacy Research, 45*(3), 295–324. doi:10.1177/1086296X13493273

Cummins, J. (1994). The acquisition of English as a second language. In K. Spangenberg-Urbschat & R. Pritchard (Eds.), *Reading instruction for ESL students.* Newark, DE: International Reading Association.Daniels, H. (1994). *Literature circles: Voice and choice in the student-centered classroom.* York, ME: Stenhouse.

Daniels, H. (2002). *Literature circles: Voice and choice in book clubs and reading groups* (2nd ed.). Portland, ME: Stenhouse.

Daniels, H., & Steineke, N. (2011). *Texts and lessons for content-area reading.* Portsmouth, NH: Heinemann.

Darch, C., Carnine, D., & Kameenuii, E. (1986). The role of graphic organizers and social structure in content area instruction. *Journal of Reading Behavior, 28*(4), 275–295.

Darling-Hammond, L., & Bransford, J. (Eds.). (2005). *Preparing teachers for a changing worlds: What teachers should learn and be able to do.* San Francisco: Jossey-Bass.

Davey, B. (1989). Assessing comprehension: Selected interactions of task and reader. *The Reading Teacher, 43*, 694–697.

DePatie-Freleng Enterprises. (1972). *The Lorax.* New York: Central Broadcasting Service.

Dewey, J. (1916). *Democracy and education.* New York: Simon and Schuster.

Discovery Education. (2015). Discovery education streaming plus. Retrieved from https://vimeo.com/discoveryeducation/review/122323352/2f74fdac2d

Doyle, K., & Dezuanni, M. (2014). Children participating in science through digital-media literacies. *Literacy Learning: The Middle Years, 22*(3), 42–54.

Duke, N.K. (2004, March). The case for informational text. *Educational Leadership*, 40–44.

Duke, N.K. (2014). *Inside information: Developing powerful readers and writers of informational text through project-based instruction.* New York: Scholastic.

Duke, N.K., & Bennett-Armistead, V.S. (2003). *Reading & writing informational text in the primary grades, research-based practices.* New York: Scholastic.

Durham, P., Ingram, J., & Contreas-Vanegas, A. (2014, November). *Becoming fluent in the language of content: Staring the conversation about content fluency in EC-6 grades.* Paper presented at the annual conference of the Association of Literacy Educators and Researchers, Delray Beach, FL.

Dymock, S. (2005). Teaching expository text structure awareness. *The Reading Teacher, 59*(2), 177–181.

Dymock, S., & Nicholson, T. (2010). "High 5!" strategies to enhance comprehension of expository text. *Reading Teacher, 64*(3), 166–178.

Education Development Center. (2012). YouthLearn Initiative. How to: Inquiry. Morino Institute.

Farnan, N., Flood, J., & Lapp, D. (1994). Comprehending through reading and writing: Six research-based instructional strategies. In K. Spangenberg-Urbschat & R. Pritchard (Eds.), *Kids come in all languages: Reading instruction for ESL students* (pp. 135–157). Newark, DE: International Reading Association.

Forehand, M. (2005). Bloom's taxonomy: Original and revised. In M. Orey (Ed.), *Emerging perspectives of learning, teaching, and technology.* Retrieved December 7, 2015, from http://projects.coe.uga.edu/epltt/index.php?title=Bloom%27s_Taxonomy

Fortuna, C. (2015). Offsetting the fears of digital applications in the classroom. Retrieved from http://www.literacyworldwide.org/blog/literacy-daily/2015/08/21/offsetting-the-fear-of-digital-applications-in-the-classroom.

Freebody, P., & Muspratt, S. (2007). Uses and effects of The Le@arning Federation's learning objects: An experimental and observational study. Retrieved from ://www.thelearningfederation.edu.au/verve/_resources/dr_report_11_02_07.pdf

Frye, E., Trathen, W., & Koppenhaver, D. (2010). Internet workshop and blog publishing: Meeting student (and teacher) learning needs to achieve best practice in the twenty-first-century social studies classroom. *Social Studies, 101*, 46–53. doi: 10.1080/0037790903284070

Gee, J.P. (1989). What is literacy? *Journal of Education, 171*(1), 18–25.

Gerber, H.P. (2009). From the FPS to the RPG: Using video games to encourage reading YAL. *ALAN Review, 36*(3), 87–91.

Harcourt, D., & Keen, D. (2012). Learner engagement: Has the child been lost in translation? *Australasian Journal of Early Childhood, 37*(3), 71–78.

Harmon, J.M., Wood, K.D., Hedrick, W.B., Vintinner, J., & Willeford. T. (2009). Interactive word walls: More than just reading the writing on the walls. *Journal of Adolescent & Adult Literacy, 52*(5), 398–408.

Harvey, S., & Daniels, H. (2009). *Comprehension and collaboration.* Portsmouth, NH: Heinemann.

Hiebert, E. (1999). *Text matters in learning to read.* CIERA Report #1-001. Ann Arbor, MI: CIERA (Center for the Improvement of Early Reading Achievement), University of Michigan School of Education. www.ciera.org

Horton, S., Lovitt, T., & Bergerud, D. (1990). The effectiveness of graphic organizers for three classifications of secondary students in content-area classes. *Journal of Learning Disabilities, 23*(1), 12–22.

Hughes-Hassell, S., & Lutz, C. (2006). What do you want to tell us about reading? A survey of the habits and attitudes of urban middle school students toward leisure reading. *Young Adult Library Services, 4*(2), 39–45.

International Reading Association. (2009). New literacies in the 21st century: A position statement of the International Reading Association. Retrieved from http://www.reading.org/Libraries/position-statements-and-resolutions/ps1067_NewLiteracies21stCentury.pdf

Ivey, G. (2002). Getting started: Manageable practices. *Educational Leadership, 60*(3), 20–23.

Jasmine, J., & Schiesl, P. (2009). The effects of word walls and word wall activities on the reading fluency of first grade students. *Reading Horizons, 49*(4), 301–304.

Kelley, M.J., & Clausen-Grace, N. (2010). Guiding students through expository text with text feature walks. *The Reading Teacher, 64,* 191–195. doi:10.1598/RT.64.3.4

Knobel, M., & Lankshear, C. (2007). *The new literacies sampler.* New York: Peter Lang, 2–17.

Korat, O., & Shamir, A. (2006). The educational electronic book as a tool for supporting children's emergent literacy in low versus middle SES groups. *Computers & Education, 50,* 110–124. doi:10.1016/j.compedu.2006.04.002

Kristo, L.V., & Bamford, R.A. (2004). *Nonfiction in focus: A comprehensive framework for helping students become independent readers and writers of nonfiction, K-6.* New York: Scholastic.

Kuhlthau, C.C., Maniotes, L.K., & Caspari, A.K. (2007). *Guided inquiry learning in the 21st century.* Libraries Unlimited.

Leu, D.J., Jr. (2002). Internet workshop: Making time for literacy. *The Reading Teacher, 55*(5), 466–472.

Leu, D.J., Jr., Coiro, J., Castek, J., Hartman, D.K., Henry, L.A., & Reinking, D. (2008). Research on instruction and assessment of the new literacies of online reading comprehension. In C.C. Block, S. Parris, & P. Afflerbach (Eds.), *Comprehension instruction: Research-based best practices.* New York: Guilford Press.

Leu, D.J., Jr., Kinzer, C.K., Coiro, J., & Cammack, D.W. (2004). Toward a theory of new literacies emerging from the internet and other information and communication technologies. In R.B. Ruddell & N. Unrau (Eds.), *Theoretical models and processes of reading* (5th ed., pp. 1570–1613). Newark, DE: International Reading Association. Retrieved from http://www.readingonline.org.ezproxy.shsu.edu/newliteracies/litindex.asp?HREF=leu/

REFERENCES

Manoli, P., & Papadopoulou, M. (2012). Graphic organizers as a reading strategy: Research findings and issues. *Creative Education, 3(3)*, 348–356.

Mason, C., Berson, M., Diem, R., Hicks, D., Lee, J., & Dralle, T. (2000). Guidelines for using technology to prepare social studies teachers. *Contemporary Issues in Technology and Teacher Education, 1*(1), 107–116.

Mayer, R.E. (2001). *Multimedia learning.* New York: Cambridge University Press.

McCormick, R., Scrimshaw, P., Li, N., & Clifford, C. (2004). CELEBRATE Evaluation report (version 2). Brussels. Retrieved from http://www.eun.org/eun.org2/eun/Include_to_content/celebrate/file/Deliverable7_2EvaluationReport02Dec04.pdf

McEneaney, J. (2006). Agent-based literacy theory. *Reading Research Quarterly, 41*(3), 352–371.

Media Smarts. (2015). The intersection of digital and media literacy. Retrieved from http://mediasmarts.ca/digital-media-literacy/general-information/digital-media-literacy-fundamentals/intersection-digital-media-literacy

Millard, E. (2003). Towards a literacy of fusion: New times, new teaching and learning? *Reading, 37,* 3–8. doi:10.1111/1467-9345.3701002

Miranda, T., Johnson, K.A., & Rossi-Williams, D. (2012). E-readers: Powering up for engagement. *Educational Leadership, 69*(9), 1–3.

Mishra, P., & Koehler, M.J. (2006). Technological pedagogical content knowledge: A framework for teacher knowledge . *Teachers College Record, 108*(6), 1017–1054.

Mohr, K. (2006). Children's choices for recreational reading: A three-part investigation of selection preferences, rationales, and processes. *Journal of Literacy Research, 38*(1), 81–104.

Mokhtari, K., Kymes, A., & Edwards, P. (2008). Assessing the new literacies of online reading comprehension: An informative interview with W. Ian O'Byrne, Lisa Zawilinski, J. Greg McVerry, and Donald J. Leu at the University of Connecticut. *Reading Teacher, 62*(4), 354–357. doi:10.1598/RT.62.4

Moll, L., Amanti, C., Neff, D., & Gonzalez, N. (1992). Funds of knowledge for teaching: Using a qualitative approach to connect homes and classrooms. *Theory Into Practice, 31*(2), 132–141.

Moss, B. (2003). *Exploring the literature of fact: Children's nonfiction trade books in the elementary classroom.* New York: Guilford Press.

National Council for the Social Studies. (1994). Curriculum standards for social studies: Time, continuity, and change – Strand 2. Retrieved from http://www.socialstudies.org/standards

Neuman, S.B., & Dwyer, J. (2009). Missing in action: Vocabulary instruction in pre-K. *The Reading Teacher, 62*(5), 384–392.

Ogle, D.M. (1986). K-W-L: A teaching model that develops active reading of expository text. *Reading Teacher, 39*, 564–570.

Olds, H.F., Schwartz, J.L., & Willie, N.A. (1980, September). *People and computers: Who teaches whom?* Newton, MA: Education Development Center.

Oregon State University. (2004). OSU extended campus: Course development: Instructional design-The Taxonomy Table. Retrieved December 7, 2015, from http://oregonstate.edu/instruct/coursedev/models/id/taxonomy/

Palinscar, A., & Brown, A.L. (1984). Reciprocal teaching of comprehension-fostering and comprehension-monitoring activities. *Cognition & Instruction, 1*(2), 117.

Pappas, C. (1993). Is narrative "primary"? Some insights from kindergartners' pretend readings of stories and inform books. *Journal of Reading Behavior, 25*, 97–129.

Pendleton, M. (2013). Through the lens: Multimodal science, math, and literacy practices in an elementary classroom. *Meridian* (10979778), *16*(1), 1–12.

Piaget, J. (1954). *To understand is to invent.* New York: Grossman.

Piaget, J., & Cook, M.T. (1952). *The origins of intelligence in children.* New York: International University Press.

Polly, D., & Brantley-Dias, L. (2009). TPACK: Where do we go now? *Tech Trends, 53*(5), 46–47.

Polly, D., & Hannafin, M.J. (2010). Reexamining technology's role in learner-centered professional development. *Educational Technology Research and Development, 58*(5), 557–571.

Roberts, T., & Billings, L. (2008). *Speak up and listen.* Asheville, NC: The National Paideia Center. Retreived from http://www.paideia.org/wp-content/uploads/2011/04/Kappen-SpeakUpListen102009.pdf

Sanacore, J., & Piro, J. (2014). Multimodalities, neuroenhancement, and literacy learning. *International Journal of Progressive Education, 10*(2), 56–72.

Santa, C., Havens, L., & Maycumber, E. (1996). *Project CRISS: Creating independence through student-owned strategies.* Dubuque, IA: Kendall/Hunt Publishing.

Schlick Noe, K.L., & Johnson, N.J. (1999). *Getting started with literature circles.* Norwood, MA: Christopher-Gordon.

Schnotz, W., & Bannert, M. (2003). Construction and interference in learning from multiple representations. *Learning and Instruction, 13*, 141–156.

Shelby-Caffey, C., Úbéda, E., & Jenkins, B. (2014). Digital storytelling revisited. *Reading Teacher, 68*(3), 191–199. doi:10.1002/trtr.1273

Shernoff, D., Csikszentmihalyi, M., Schneider, B., & Shernoff, E. (2003). Student engagement in high school classrooms from the perspective of flow theory. *School Psychology Quarterly, 18*(2), 158–176.

Shine.com. (2014). *Social and digital skills must haves for new age employees*. Retrieved from http://info.shine.com/article/social-and-digital-skills-musthaves-for-new-age-employees/1399.html

Shulman, L.S. (2005). Signature pedagogies in the disciplines. *Daedalus, 134*, 52–59.

Snow, C., Burns, S., & Griffin, P. (1998). *Preventing reading difficulty in young children.* Washington, DC: National Research Council.

Spires, H., Hervey, L., Morris, G., & Stelpflug, C. (2012). Energizing project-based inquiry: Middle grade students read, write, and create videos. *Journal of Adolescent & Adult Literacy, 55*, 483–493. doi:10.1002/JAAL.00058

Stahl, S.A., & Nagy, W.E. (2006). *Teaching word meanings.* Mahwah, NJ: Erlbaum.

Staudt, C., & Forman, G. (2014). *Sensing science: Temperature and heat readiness for early elementary students.* Retrieved from https://concord.org/publications/newsletter/2014-spring/sensing-science

Straits, W., & Nichols, S. (2005). Literature circles for science. *Science and Children, 44*(3), 52– 55.

Thomas, A. (2011). Towards a transformative digital literacies pedagogy. *Nordic Journal of Digital Literacy, 6*(01-02), 89–101

Todd, D. (2008). *Timetoast, a website for creating timelines.* Retrieved from https://www.timetoast.com/

Tompkins, G.E. (2005). *Language arts: Patterns of practice* (6th ed.). Upper Saddle River, NJ: Pearson.

Tyner, K. (2014). *Literacy in a digital world: Teaching and learning in the age of information.* Florence, KY: Routledge Publishers.

Valdes, G., Bunch, G., Snow, C., Lee, C., & Matos, L. (2005). *Enhancing the development of student's language(s).* Edited by L. Darling-Hammond & J. Bransford. San Francisco: Jossey-Bass.

Van DeVeghe, R. (2006). What is engaged learning? *English Journal, 95*(3), 88–91.

Van Rose, S. (2004). *Eyewitness volcano & earthquake.* New York: DK Publishing, Inc.

Walsh, M. (2010). Multimodal literacy: What does it mean for classroom practice? *Australian Journal of Language and Literacy, 33*(3), 211–239.

Wasik, B.A. (2006). Building vocabulary one word at a time. *Young Children, 61*(6), 70–78.

Weaver, C. (2002). *Reading process and practice* (3rd ed.). Portsmouth, NH: Heinemann.

Wolfersberger, M.E., Reutzel, D.R., Sudweeks, R., & Fawson, P.C. (2004). Developing and validating the classroom literacy environmental profile (CLEP): A tool for examining the "print richness" of early childhood and elementary classrooms. *Journal of Literacy Research, 36*(2), 211–272. doi:10.1207/s15548430jlr3602_4

Zipke, M. (2013). Teachers' thoughts on e-readers in the elementary school classroom. *Education & Information Technologies, 18*(3), 421–441.

Literature Cited

Carbone, E. (2007). *Blood on the river: Jamestown, 1607.* New York: Puffin Books.

Sroda, A. (2000). Wings for the king. *Drama Magazine for Young People, 60*(2), 41.

Van Allsburg, C. (1981). *Jumanji.* Boston: Houghton Mifflin Co.

Van Allsburg, C. (1985). *Polar express.* Boston: Houghton Mifflin Co.

CPSIA information can be obtained
at www.ICGtesting.com
Printed in the USA
LVHW062324070420
652200LV00001B/1

9 781465 292921